CHANNELING CHILDREN

SEX STEREOTYPING IN PRIME-TIME TV

An Analysis by
WOMEN ON WORDS AND IMAGES

Phyllis AlRoy
Joan Bartl
Rogie Bender
Pryde Brown
Cynthia Eaton
Carol Portnoi Jacobs
Ann Stefan

Written by Betty Miles

With the help of
    Ann Bruner
    Sue Horowitz
    Paul I. Jacobs
    Cecelia Jacobowitz
    Barbara Kirsh
    Deloris Sanders
    Robin Liebemann Wallack
    Gita Wilder

Cover by: Suzi Kittredge

Library of Congress No. 75-568
ISBN 0-9600724-2-X

Table of Contents

91897

Part One

INTRODUCTION

Every parent knows, along with the experts, that television exerts a powerful influence upon children. Children do learn from TV. This booklet describes a study of sex stereotyping — the presentation of outmoded, incorrect or prejudicial messages about how men and women behave — as it existed in the most popular early evening programs of the 1973 and 1974 viewing seasons. These programs, considered "family entertainment," influence the role expectations of millions of young children who watch them.

The study was made by an action group, Women on Words and Images, whose prior research documented the extent of sex stereotyping in children's school readers. Their findings, published in 1972 in a booklet, *Dick and Jane as Victims* (14), showed that 75 percent of textbook stories focused on male characters. In addition, the report showed that those females who *were* portrayed in the readers displayed passivity, domesticity and dependence, while males were almost always drawn, in text and in illustration, as aggressive, independent, capable and successful under pressure. This study by Women on Words and Images, along with subsequent studies, showed that school books designed to teach reading skills were also teaching young children to have stereotyped expectations about the lives of men and women, boys and girls.

As a consequence of the publication of *Dick and Jane as Victims* and other studies, educators, textbook publishers, authors, illustrators and parents have become aware of the pervasiveness of sex stereotyping in children's school books and the negative effects it can have on the self-esteem and expectations of all young children. Currently, changes toward greater

1

equality in the portrayal of males and females have been made in books, and there is a growing awareness of the importance of equal rights in education, supported in part by the issuance in 1974 of the Title IX Guidelines to the Higher Education Act of 1972. These guidelines, though they do not deal with textbook content, do direct schools in America to move toward equal treatment of all students.

Because of the importance of television in the lives of children, Women on Words and Images moved in 1973 from the study of textbooks to a study of television programs, choosing to focus on those ostensibly adult dramatic shows aired in prime evening time, and viewed by millions of children before their bedtime. In addition to being billed as family entertainment, these shows were also selected because they present real people (not animated figures) moving through situations that, whether historical or contemporary, exaggerated or naturalistic, are nonetheless understood to be dramatizations of "real life" by the viewer.

In the 1973 viewing season, sixteen programs were observed, and data on the number and occupation of female and male characters, and on positive and negative behaviors, including such traits as competence and aggression, were recorded. In addition, plot summaries were written from notes made while the programs were being viewed, and the summaries were revised immediately after the programs with the help of tape recordings made during the episodes. In the 1974 season, reports of the programs were descriptive only, and no statistical check-lists were kept.

Thus, the present study has two major parts: a statistical survey of one year's top-rated dramatic programs; and descriptions of sample episodes from the top-rated shows of two seasons. While programs on television come and go with devastating frequency, it is the assumption of this study that the statistical and descriptive analysis of the particular dramatic programs viewed during two specific seasons can be taken as representative of the dramatic programs on television for seasons to come. In fact, a common critical complaint is that change in television program content comes slowly from one season to another, and that a single popular dramatic format

2

A BRIEF REVIEW OF THE RESEARCH ON CHILDREN AND TELEVISION

Three basic questions are raised in the existing research on television and children: (1) about exposure — how much time do children spend watching? (2) about content — *what* are they watching, and what messages are they receiving? (3) about effects — in what, if any, ways, does television create, reinforce or alter the world-view, *and the behavior,* of children?

Many gaps exist in the available research on these questions, particularly on topic (3), the effects of viewing television on the subsequent behavior of children. Obviously, any attempt to show a causal relationship between what children see on the screen and how they behave afterwards is difficult because, in real life, so many complex factors — from birth order to condition of the TV set to family tensions to school experience — might also be cited to explain why a child who watched Kung Fu on a particular night kicked his brother when the show was over.

Nevertheless, most people who live with children don't need a statistician to tell which way the twig is bending. Children, we know, *do* imitate, and television, because it is an important part of their lives, is a prime source of their imitations. Children do ask for the cereals and toys they see advertised on TV; they do learn to sing commercials and repeat punchlines *ad nauseum;* they do (though fortunately not all of them) jump their bikes over astounding barriers and join the nation-wide epidemic of broken arms that followed Evel Knievel's abortive leap across the Snake River Canyon.

A summary of major research about children and television

7

would indicate that (1) children watch a lot of television; (2) that many children's programs and adult situation dramas involve violence; (3) that there is some — how much is unclear — causal relationship between violence on television and social behavior on the part of children.

A brief review of some major studies of children's relationship to television follows. The studies described were selected because they illustrate kinds of research in the field, and because their outcomes are typical of other studies' findings or relevant to this one. A bibliography of selected studies on children and television will be found at the end of this booklet. Studies mentioned in this chapter are cited on page 75.

Exposure

Much of what is known about children's television viewing today derives from studies made by Schramm, Lyle and Parker (12) between 1958 and 1960. These researchers conducted a total of eleven studies involving 6,000 children and 2,000 parents in five different locations. They used questionnaires, interviews and diaries to study the relationship between age, socio-economic class and viewing behavior and to determine the uses children made of television.

Schramm and his associates found that frequent viewing begins for most children at age three and remains relatively high until they are about twelve. In the early teens there is typically a decline. With marriage, viewing increases and remains stable throughout the adult years, increasing still further as grown children leave home.

Schramm and his associates report that throughout childhood and into the early teens, television is the dominant form of media usage. That is, children spend more time watching television than they do reading books, magazines, newspapers or comic books, listening to the radio, or going to the movies. Children from blue-collar families tend to watch more television than children from white-collar families. Blacks and Mexican-Americans, both children and adults, tend to view more than whites. Children with high I. Q.'s tend to view more than children with low I. Q.'s in early childhood, but the trend reverses with increasing age.

8

A replication of the Schramm research by Lyle and Hoffman (7) in 1971 shows many of the same findings. Lyle and Hoffman conclude that television is a major activity for most children. A report from the Surgeon General's Advisory Committee on Television and Social Behavior, a research group which will be discussed more fully in the following section, again confirms the Schramm data.

Content

What do television viewers see when they watch? Since concern over violence is an important issue in the United States, many research studies have focused on the amount of violence shown on TV. Other studies have focused on the distinctions between reality and fantasy on television, the distortions and misinformation of advertisements, and, most relevant to the present study, the stereotyped treatment of national and ethnic groups and occupational and sex roles.

In 1968, the Surgeon General's Advisory Committee on Television and Social Behavior funded twenty-three separate research studies, all of them addressing the question of whether a causal connection exists between the viewing of violence on television and the appearance of aggressive behavior in children. One of the most comprehensive and interesting of the studies is that of Gerbner (4) who made a detailed content analysis of one week of prime-time and Saturday morning viewing in the fall of 1969, and compared it with similar studies he had made in 1967 and 1968. Gerbner found a great deal of violence in the programs his researchers monitored. A communications specialist, Gerbner sees television violence as symbolic, a representation of the power structure of society. "Violence and television action tend to be the prerogative of a male free of responsibilities," he reports, observing that about 75 percent of the characters in programs monitored were middle-class American males, unmarried and in the prime of life. "Meanwhile," he adds, "American women are generally portrayed as exuding sexual attraction, as mates in marriage, or both; as lacking in social power and influence; and as much more likely to be the objects of victimization than men."

Other findings of the Gerbner study include the limited

9

variety of roles played by women as compared with those taken by men, and the tendency of women involved in television violence to be its victims. Gerbner concludes, "If the ability to be violent and to avoid victimization symbolically represents the possession of power and influence, then women are clearly depicted as less endowed than men with these assets."3

Some of the most effective monitoring of television content has been carried out by political action groups seeking supporting evidence for their demands for change in broadcasting practices. The best known and most successful such group is the Boston-based Action for Children's Television (ACT) which has conducted content analyses of children's shows and of their commercials, and commissioned studies on mothers' attitudes toward children's television programs and commercials, the treatment of black and other minority groups on network children's television, and alternate methods of financing children's programming. ACT won an important victory in 1972 when three major drug companies agreed to stop advertising vitamins on television shows for children. In the same year, an ACT-sponsored study (2) of Saturday morning television in the Boston area found a cultural sex bias in commercials. Forty-nine commercials contained males only, while sixteen contained females only. Characters in toy ads were found to be identified by stereotyped sex-role, girls playing with dolls and boys with cars.

The Washington, D. C. chapter of NOW conducted an intensive monitoring of one week of programming by a television station in the Washington metropolitan area in 1973 to gather statistical information on the number of males and females and the incidence of their appearances on the channel during the week. Data for six kinds of television shows were analyzed, and results recorded for each; the most detailed analysis was made of commercials.

Out of a total of 2,750 ads monitored and analyzed, a total of 33 percent was devoted to domestic products — food, beverages, household products — and another 20 percent to personal hygiene products. About 80 percent of the commercials used a narrator's voice over the picture, and in 93 percent of the cases this voice was male. The group's report (9) concluded that women and men were presented differently in the commercials analyzed, as in all the shows studied, and that "each sex was shown in those roles and activities that are traditional." The researchers found that women's professional status was virtually ignored in the commercials and that women shown working outside the home were most often found in traditional "women's occupations."

A similar analysis of roles portrayed by men and women in television advertising was carried out by the New York City chapter of NOW in 1972 (8). The conclusions, based on 1,241 commercials aired during a randomly-selected five-day period, were similar to those of the Washington study: "Household functions are overwhelmingly performed by women . . . By contrast, non-household functions are overwhelmingly performed by males . . . Women in commercials are generally depicted as primarily engaged in household tasks, as domestic adjuncts of males. They are also shown as emotionally dependent on and subservient to men. Few women are shown as intelligent."

Effect

Why are political action groups so concerned about stereotyped behavior on television? And why was a national commission established to study how television violence affects viewers? Perhaps because so little is really known about the effects of television on its audience, particularly on those young viewers for whom TV is a major activity. Schramm (12) and his colleagues concluded, after surveying 6,000 children in the early 60's, that

For some children, under some conditions, some television is harmful. For other children under the same conditions, or for the same children under other conditions, it may be beneficial. For most children, under most conditions, most television is probably neither harmful nor particularly beneficial.

Despite the newer and more sophisticated studies which have appeared in the research literature during the past decade, the recently published summary volume of the Surgeon General's Report (13) finds that we cannot conclusively measure the

11

effects of television.

The complexities of developmental process in childhood and adolescence and the variations from one individual to another make it difficult to predict the effects of any single carefully controlled stimulus upon behavior and impossible to predict fully the effects of the wide variety of visual and auditory stimuli offered in television programs.

Nevertheless, studies continue to be made, and, despite the obvious difficulties, inferences can be drawn from them.

Children's Television Workshop was established in 1968 in order to develop and present a daily TV show for preschoolers that would educate while it entertained. From the start, research and evaluation of CTW's program, Sesame Street, was carried out by Educational Testing Service. The same evaluation group stayed on to research a later CTW program, The Electric Company, a show with similar goals, but aimed at children in the primary grades with reading difficulties.

Using a large number of subjects in five different locations, researchers pre-tested and post-tested children for their achievement of goals ranging from "recognizing and naming the letters of the alphabet" to recognizing "that in certain situations it is beneficial for two or more individuals to work together toward a common goal." In addition, the researchers interviewed parents and teachers, and kept records of viewing behavior. Both evaluations came to similar conclusions; they found that television can be an effective tool for teaching children many of the things that the programs intended them to learn, and that the amount of learning was a function of the amount of viewing, and of the amount of exposure a particular goal received on the show.

Critics of the Sesame Street evaluation have downgraded the *type* of learning measured and achieved, calling it "rote." Assuming that television can and does convey factual information that can be easily memorized, they ask, what about its more subtle effects on attitudes, beliefs and behavior?

A large body of research literature is devoted to the effects of television violence upon children, some of it summarized in the Surgeon General's Report, and some initiated by the Surgeon General's Committee.

The experimental studies that provide the most persuasive evidence that television *can* alter behavior are derived from the theory and research of Albert Bandura (1). Bandura's work has produced and generated a series of studies of children's reactions to filmed or televised episodes of aggressive or violent behavior. The form of most of these studies is quite similar. Subjects are observed, tested or interviewed before the showing of a selected set of films. They are then subjected to the experimental conditions, one group being exposed to violent viewing matter while the other is given a non-violent or neutral stimulus. Observations, tests and measurements are made at the end of the viewing period. by albert Bandura

For the most part, the studies show that some children do indeed model their own behavior upon behavior they see on television. Usually, they show an increase in the number of aggressive acts, hostility of vocabulary or number or intensity of negative responses to a projected test on the part of a few experimental subjects. stop

Because it is difficult to generalize from laboratory experiments, Liefer and Roberts (6) studied 271 children from five to eighteen as they watched six half-hour episodes of television shows chosen for their violent content. The researchers found a significant age difference in children's understanding of the motivations of television characters and the consequences of their violence. Kindergarten children were least able to understand the motivations and consequences; older children understood better, but understood motive better than consequence. The researchers concluded that children as young as five do not really understand either motives or consequences as they are currently portrayed on television.

Liefer and Roberts found minimal evidence that children's aggressive responses changed as a result of exposure to television. Although there seemed to be no sex differences in children's responses to the shows, at all age levels boys were consistently more likely to choose aggressive responses than girls.

The Surgeon General's Report provides a clear summary of

evidence obtained from experimental studies of the effects of aggressive television content on children. Violence on television, it states, *can* induce imitative behavior in children shortly after exposure. Under some conditions, television violence can instigate an increase in aggressive acts. However, the accumulated evidence does not support the hypothesis that television violence has a uniformly adverse effect, nor does it support the conclusion that negative effects apply to the majority of children. There is strong evidence to suggest that television violence can have adverse effects on a *subset* of the children who watch such shows, and ongoing research is beginning to give a clearer picture of the types of children who might be adversely affected.

Finally, in recent years some researchers have turned their interest to the use of television to promote "prosocial," or positive, behavior. Friedrich and Stein (3) conducted a study of ninety-three pre-school children in a nursery school program, showing them one of three types of television programs each day during the middle four weeks of the nine-week session: "Aggressive cartoons" (Batman and Superman) "prosocial programs" (Mister Rogers Neighborhood) and "neutral films" (an assortment of films chosen because they had neither violent nor prosocial content). Children's free play was observed prior to, during and after the showing of the films.

The researchers found that children who had initially been rated above average in aggression followed their viewing of aggressive material with an increase in interpersonal aggression. Children exposed to prosocial programs showed higher levels of self-regulatory behaviors than did the children who watched the neutral films. Interestingly, the increase in prosocial behavior was not accompanied by a decrease in aggressive behavior; the new behaviors were, rather, in addition to those already displayed. Friedrich and Stein concluded that they had seen evidence of the generalization of television effects to behavior without having observed any direct imitation of the TV programs. In all, the experiment lends support to the authors' initial contention that "the medium has as much potential to teach children positive forms of social behavior as it has to teach them aggressive and antisocial behavior."

14

Recent research by Liebert (5) supports this contention. Controlled studies of children fearful of dogs show that eight out of nine who saw a ten-minute film of a young child overcoming fear as an older child played confidently with a dog were immediately willing to approach a real German Shepherd, while children who had not seen the film retained their fear.

Another film about a four-year-old girl who fearfully watched an eight-year-old boy climb into the dentist's chair for a cleaning, and then followed him into the chair herself was shown to a group of children whose mothers said they were afraid of the dentist. After viewing the film, these children were shown pictures of a dentist and two other community helpers and asked which they would like to visit at work. The dentist received a vote of confidence of 4.2 on a scale of six from children who had viewed the film, while a control group of nonviewers rated the dentist 2.6 and a group who saw another film rated him 2.2.

A film about nursery school behavior (O'Connor, 10) was shown to twelve children who had exhibited marked withdrawal symptoms upon entering nursery school. In each of the film's eleven scenes, a child first observes an activity and then participates after receiving positive encouragement to do so. The six children who saw the film markedly increased the number and quality of their interactions with the other nursery school children. The other six children, who had seen a film about dolphins, were as withdrawn in the nursery school setting as they had been at the start of the study.

Summary (Conclusion)

The precise nature of the effects of television viewing on any given child or group of children is probably not predictable, but the literature does indicate some general principles. It is clear, for example, that television viewing is an important activity for the vast majority of American children from as early an age as two or three. We know, too, that for many children television is the major vehicle for contact with the world outside family and home. Studies have indicated that children learn from television — in some cases the very things that the producers of a program, or a commercial, want them to learn; in other cases lessons that are unintended. Studies also show that children sometimes model their own behavior after behavior they have observed on television, either in accord with the viewed behavior or in opposition to it. As Liebert (5) summarizes,

> Quite simply, any steady diet of television will have a powerful influence on children. Its effect is, at least in part, the inevitable, natural consequence of observing behavior in others. Modeling — in which a child learns from witnessing the actions of other persons — is a cornerstone in social development. Television, by its very nature, brainwashes children in that it shapes the way they view the world and the kind of people they will be. We cannot rid ourselves of its influence. . . (8)"

There is no argument among researchers about the potential of the television medium. These studies are impressive in their conclusions that television can exert a powerful influence on the thoughts, feelings, attitudes, beliefs and perhaps the behavior of young viewers.

AN ANALYSIS OF SEX STEREOTYPING IN PRIME-TIME PROGRAMS

The basic question of this study is, <u>What is television telling our children about the masculine and feminine roles of adults?</u> To find answers, the study was organized in the following ways:

1. Top-rated, prime-time dramatic shows aimed at a family audience were chosen for observation.

Since children learn behaviors more directly from real than from cartoon characters, children's programs which make extensive use of animated figures or puppets were ruled out. And since adult behavior was central to the question, dramatic programs focusing on adult interaction were the obvious choice for observation. (Variety and game shows were eliminated because they focus on performers rather than on character actors, and have a rigid format which precludes a range of behaviors).

Neilson ratings for the first week of November, 1973 (a date that allowed for an initial shake-down of the new season's shows) were used to find the most widely-viewed shows between the hours of 7:30 p.m. and 9:30 p.m., when a majority of children are awake and, according to statistical evidence, watching TV. The sixteen shows selected for study fell into two categories: adventure shows (Cannon, Kung Fu, Adam-12, Hawaii Five-O) and situation comedy (Maude, Sanford and Son, Temperature's Rising, Adam's Rib, All in the Family, Diana, Mash, Mary Tyler Moore, The Waltons, The Brady Bunch, Lotsa Luck and The Girl with Something Extra).

2. Programs selected were viewed by trained observers, who recorded data on prepared forms.

Seven two-person teams, each including a member of Women on Words and Images and another woman aware of the group's position but not directly involved in its work, were involved in data collection.

Three training sessions were held to clarify the research process and unify the coding procedure. At the first session, the project was explained, shows were assigned, and sample coding sheets and instructions (see Appendix) given out. Each observer was assigned to view the same episode of That Girl, a program not included in the study. At the second session, recording experiences were compared and the coding system refined. For the final session, observers watched an episode of their assigned program and compared data with the teammate.

Each observer team viewed and recorded data from at least three episodes of two or three shows. For each episode, the viewing team watched and took notes (paying attention to visual as well as verbal data) separately, then came together to listen to an audio tape of the episode.* Jointly, they described every scene on a standard form (see Appendix) and recorded the number, age, sex and occupation of major and minor characters. (A character was designated "major" if the person played a regular part on each episode or was a featured guest on a particular episode; the character was called "minor" if the role was peripheral to the plot, like that of a neighbor who appears only to borrow a cup of sugar or a waitress who carries food to the main characters in a restaurant).

Finally, for each scene described, observers tallied behaviors, and noted the sex of the person acting out the behavior, on a rating form describing nineteen behaviors (see Appendix).

3. The data were analyzed, and conclusions were drawn. Summaries of program episodes were written. An analysis of commercials accompanying the programs was made.

Results of the study follow.

---

*As in all studies, observer bias must be assumed to affect the data to some extent. The concern over perceived stereotyping on TV that prompted the study may have influenced the observers and it is important to keep their advocacy stance in mind when reading the data.

Male-Female Ratio

More males than females appear on all shows analyzed. Large differences in number of male and female characters are evident when adventure shows are compared with situation comedies.

TABLE 1 Major Male and Female Characters — All Shows			
	Male	Female	Total
Adventure	23	4	27
Situation Comedy	63	52	115
Total — All Shows	86	56	142

Sixty-one percent of major characters in all shows analyzed are male, but in adventure shows males are 85 percent of the major characters. In situation comedy shows males represent 55 percent of major characters.

Similar ratios are obtained when the male and female minor characters are counted.

TABLE 2 Minor Male and Female Characters — All Shows			
	Male	Female	Total
Adventure	11	6	17
Situation Comedy	65	50	115
Total — All Shows	76	56	132

Male and Female Occupations

Table 3 lists male occupations ranging from architect to writer, and female occupations ranging from cleaning woman to volunteer. Nearly twice the number of occupations shown were held by major male characters on all shows as by major female characters.

TABLE 3
Occupation By Sex — All Shows

Male Occupations	Female Occupations
architect	cleaning woman — maid
bartender	clerk: filing, store, bank
butcher	congresswoman
chief of state	dancer
criminal	editor
demolition expert	*farm worker
detective	housekeeper (paid)
doctor	housewife
driver: bus, taxi, truck, limosine,	lab technician
airport ground	*landlady
factory worker	*lawyer
farmer	*librarian
*farm worker	matron
foreman	model
gambler	nurse: practical, registered, military
governor	prostitute
guard: bodyguard, prison, airport,	*radio operator
military, business	receptionist
hairstylist — barber	*religious worker
judge	*reporter
junk dealer	*saleswoman
*landlord	*secretary
*lawyer	*singer
longshoreman	stewardess
*librarian	*store owner
maitre de	teacher: art, ballet, drama
masseur	*television producer, assistant
mechanic	volunteer worker
musician	*waitress
photographer	
pilot	
policeman — sheriff	
psychiatrist	
public relations	
religious worker	
*salesman	
servant	
ship captain	
sharpshooter	
*singer	
stage manager	
*store owner	
student	
tailor	
television: producer, announcer, crew	
veterinarian	
*waiter	
welder	
writer	
*yeoman — secretary	*occupations held jointly by both sexes.

Occupational sex stereotyping is a fact of prime-time TV life. Starred on Table 3 are the few occupations which were held by both sexes in the shows observed. Now that the husband-wife lawyer team of Adam's Rib is no longer debating on television, Mary Tyler Moore remains the notable exception: *a* central female character whose work alongside male colleagues is central to the plots of a series. Other work performed by both females and males is not central. For example, women have been seen as reporters on several programs, though only in minor roles, and outnumbered by male reporters.

Economic Patterns

Among the eight shows in the study which focused on families, a variety of family economic patterns was observed. The occupations of each adult family member were recorded in order to examine each member's contribution to the family's economic condition.

TABLE 4 Wage Earners by Sex — Eight Family Shows			
	Male	Female	Total
Wage earner	9	3	12
Non-wage earner	3	7	10

The families studied support themselves in quite different ways. In The Brady Bunch, the father is an architect who supports his wife and their six children (all from previous marriages) as well as a fulltime domestic employee. The wife shares employer status over the domestic worker, although the father is clearly the only source of family income.

A similar situation with respect to domestic help occurs on Maude. Walter and Maude are both presented as employers of the paid domestic worker, although Walter is the only consistent wage earner in the family. Maude's appearance as a real-estate saleswoman occured on one episode only.

The Waltons is the presentation of an extended family in the depression era. The father works at odd jobs to keep the family supplied with bare essentials. His parents live with the family and contribute to the family income occasionally, as the children do in one instance. The mother of the family does not work outside the home.

In Lotsa Luck, a son is the sole support of his mother, sister and brother-in-law.

In the three All in the Family episodes studied, a different pattern of female economic dependency appears. Edith Bunker, the mother, is a totally dependent housewife. Her daughter Gloria and her husband live with the Bunkers and are thus dependent in a limited way, but Gloria works to support her husband while he attends college.

In Sanford and Son, The Girl with Something Extra, and Adam's Rib, all adult family members are shown contributing to total family income.

Thus, while a variety of family vocational patterns is shown, it is clear that married women and mothers on television do not support themselves financially in the majority of cases. Independent financial status is left to single women like Mary Tyler Moore.

Male/Female Behaviors

Since more men than women appear on all programs studied, it is natural that more male than female behaviors are recorded. The following table shows the distribution by sex of 2,035 behaviors noted, and compares behaviors on adventure shows with those on situation comedy programs.

TABLE 5 Number of Behaviors, By Sex — Adventure and Situation Comedy			
	Male	Male (percent of total)	Female
Adventure	424	70	172
Situation	850	60	590
Total	1274	63	761

TABLE 6	
Programs with Most Male Behaviors	
Program	Percent Male Behavior
Mash	87
Sanford and Son	82
Hawaii Five-O	81

TABLE 7	
Programs with Least Male Behaviors	
Program	Percent Male Behavior
The Brady Bunch	36
Mary Tyler Moore	41
Adam's Rib	41

All characters observed display more negative than positive behaviors overall — a rather grim finding for a survey of "entertainment." (See Appendix for table of behaviors considered positive and negative).

TABLE 8	
Negative Behaviors — All Shows	
Type of Show	Negative Behavior (percent)
Adventure	50
Situation Comedy	66
All Shows	61

However, when negative behaviors are classified by sex, females are shown in *more* instances of negative behavior than males.

TABLE 9		
Negative Behaviors by Sex		
Type of Show	Percent of Total Male Behaviors	Percent of Total Female Behaviors
Adventure	27	82
Situation Comedy	69	61
All Shows	59	66

Perhaps the most interesting finding on male/female behaviors is in the area of competence. A study of sex-role stereotypes by Rosenkrantz and Vogel (11) indicates that there is strong agreement between the sexes about behaviors seen as typically male or typically female. A list of traits that were identified as male includes: independent, objective, logical, worldly, skilled in business, knows the way the world works, makes decisions easily, acts as a leader, self-confident, not dependent. Most of these traits can be subsumed under the label "Competence." The table below shows that the television shows studied reinforce the stereotype of competence as a male trait in adventure shows, though women display a higher percentage of competence in situation comedy programs. Of course, since many more men than women are featured on all shows, competence is more frequently seen as a male trait.

TABLE 10 Male and Female Competence — All Shows				
Type of Show	Competent Behaviors — Male		Competent Behaviors — Female	
	Number	Percent	Number	Percent
Adventure	194	46	23	14
Situation Comedy	104	12	108	17
All Shows	298	22	131	18

Incompetence, as rated in this study, does not mean the simple absence of competent behavior; it means the direct bungling of opportunity, the real mistake, the obvious act of doing something badly. Women on the shows studied spent 20 percent of their total behaviors in incompetent acts. Men, on the other hand, were incompetent for only 9 percent of their total behaviors. Put another way, a woman's behavior was more than twice as likely to show incompetence than a man's.

TABLE 11 Male and Female Incompetence — All Shows				
Type of Show	Incompetent Behaviors — Male		Incompetent Behaviors — Female	
	Number	Percent	Number	Percent
Adventure	14	3	53	31
Situation	103	12	103	16
All Shows	117	9	156	20

Finally, observers recorded the ways men and women expressed anger. While 22 percent of women on the television programs studied expressed anger through sarcasm or some indirect form of put-down, 45 percent of the men on these programs expressed their anger by putting down somebody else.

Commercials

Some children who watch television steadily probably understand, like most adults, that commercials are not really part of the shows into which they intrude. Some children hear their families discount the messages of the commercials and come to understand that the wise, comforting voice selling a particular spaghetti sauce is not necessarily telling the full truth about it.

However, commercials are part of the overall television viewing experience. And unfortunately, for many children as well as some adults, the commercial message appears to be just one more piece of information from the television set — information that is presented more explicitly and more persuasively than most. Many children are not as able as more experienced adults to separate truth in advertising from fiction, particularly when the fiction is presented in catchy music, compelling words and striking images.

A case against commercials can be made on many grounds: for their distortion of fact, their easy equation of acquisition with happiness, their simplistic answers to peoples' serious problems. Here, the concern is with sex stereotyping in television commercials only.

Two hundred and fourteen commercials were viewed during the study of the sixteen dramatic shows. Statistically, the difference between the number of women and men appearing in all the commercials was small, and women had more speaking parts in them than men.

TABLE 12 Male and Female Characters — Commercials		
	Appearance	Speaking Parts
Males	399	164
Females	343	195

However, what the women are saying perhaps explains why they talk so much. In many cases, women function as demonstrators of a housekeeping product, describing how the mopping or cooking or cleaning goes more smoothly when the product is used. These women demonstrators' concern is focused on issues like how white the laundry gets, how shiny the floors are, how mirror-like the dishes become in the dishwasher.

But when an authoritative voice-over is heard, summarizing the products' virtues and urging their purchase and use, the voice is almost always male.

TABLE 13 Sex of Voice-Over — Commercials		
Sex	Number of Times Heard	Percent
Male	258	96
Female	11	4

In the commercials observed, as in dramatic programs, nearly twice as many men than women were shown as employed people, and the variety of men's occupations was far greater than women's.

TABLE 14 Male/Female Employment — Commercials		
Sex	Number Employed	Number of Occupations
Male	87	40
Female	44	21

Although women on most family shows like All in the Family, The Brady Bunch, The Waltons, and Little House on the Prairie are relegated to domestic tasks, they are also seen as loving mothers, wise counselors, supportive wives. They are stereotyped, but they are seen as persons beyond their roles. Women in the commercials, however, have no time beyond their thirty-to sixty-second stints of mopping, scrubbing, cooking or serving for talking about anything beyond the toilet bowl cleaner or the spaghetti sauce.

Women in the commercials are shown proudly serving

convenience foods, or listening deferentially to a white-coated "scientist's" explanation of the newest washday miracle, or showing inept husbands the right way to scrub floors. As Table 16 shows, they are less frequently found in paying jobs and more frequently found caring for the sick.

TABLE 15
Occupation by Sex — Commercials

Male occupation	Number	Female occupation	Number
businessman	8	housewife	30
doctor	8	secretary	9
auto mechanic	6	stewardess	7
personality	6	personality	5
waiter	5	teacher	4
construction worker	5	waitress	3
steelworker	3	columnist	2
appliance repairman	3	Avon saleswoman	1
oil driller	3	bank teller	1
television cameraman	3	business executive	1
butler	2	chorus girl	1
garage manager	2	flower seller	1
race car driver	2	interviewer	1
ski instructor	2	model	1
air traffic controller	1	Mother Nature	1
band member	1	nun	1
breeder	1	singer	1
bulldozer operator	1	technician	1
chef	1		
clerk	1		
coffee company owner	1		
co-pilot	1		
doorman	1		
druggist	1		
farmer	1		
mailman	1		
museum guard	1		
nuclear scientist	1		
photographer	1		
plumber	1		
police chief	1		
Santa Claus	1		
security guard	1		
store owner	1		
stunt driver	1		
tour guide	1		

Next, a summary was made of what the major characters in these commercials were *actually doing*. Here, striking contrasts appeared between the activities men and women perform in the world of commercials.

TABLE 16 Male/Female Activities — Commercials		
Activity	Male	Female
Work at paying job	35	17
Children at play	19	2
Adults at play or sport (camping, fishing, photographing)	16	2
Physician-type authority	11	0
Sick adult being cared for	8	0
Eating	7	2
Driving a car	6	1
Admiring or buying a car	4	1
Housework (mopping, scrubbing, washing, doing dishes, cleaning)	4	23
Cooking	1	9
Serving others	0	8
Shopping	0	9
Caring for children	0	3
Caring for sick adult	0	8

Along with their routine tasks, women of the commercials have another crucial responsibility: making themselves attractive. Women greatly outnumber men in this basic activity.

TABLE 17		
Male/Female Care of Self — Commercials		
Activity	Male	Female
Attention to appearance	1	23
Attention to cleanliness (deodorant, shampoo, soap)	3	8

It is interesting to note that, of the children shown on prime-time ads, nineteen boys were pictured at play and only three girls. Stereotypes of activity, competence and success seem to be passed on to the next generation by the writers of commercials.

The foregoing analysis of commercials makes it clear that on television advertisements men, or male voices, are dominant and authoritative. Men work more, play more and eat more — and they get sick more. Women are, first of all, concerned with their appearance — after that, they do housework and shop and cook and care for others, including those sick males. So the commercials interrupt the stereotyped prime-time shows with similar stereotypes of their own. Perhaps the only difference is that, on the commercials, the stereotypes are somewhat more explicit.

Summary

Children learn from watching the actions of other persons. Every night, at prime-time, millions of American children watch grown women and men relating to each other in television dramas about "real life." What do they see?

To summarize: they see, overall, more men than women on their television screens; on the exciting adventure shows, they see nearly six times as many men. The men they see work in diverse occupations, nearly twice the number of those held by women characters. They see three-quarters of the adult males in shows about families contributing to family support, and only one-third of adult females helping with this support.

Surprisingly, all adult characters observed showed more negative than positive characters, so that child viewers may sense an overall tone of grimness in adult life as portrayed on the screen. But the behavior of women characters is even more negative than that of men; thus, while fewer women are seen at all, children see a higher percentage of those that do appear performing negative behaviors. Children see that more male than female behaviors show competence, and that more female behaviors display *in*competence. On the commercials, children see women taking care of their houses, their families, their shopping and their own appearance, while men work and play harder and provide the voice of authority for the purchasing decisions women make.

The prime-time message of the television screen is that there are more men around, and that they are dominant, authoritative and competent. While neither sex displays a majority of positive behaviors, women come off showing even more negative behaviors than men. Archie may be mean-spirited, but he is dominant and authoritatively mean, a master of the put-down, as well. Edith is incompetent, dependent, and victim. The few times when she does successfully solve a problem, she belittles herself. Together, they serve as models of adult life in contemporary America for the children who sit in front of their television sets, laughing along with the laugh track at the way men and women get on together.

LOOKING TOWARD A NEW SEASON: CHANGING THE STEREOTYPES

Adults may feel a sense of hopelessness and frustration at the pervasiveness of the sex stereotypes children see on television. What can they do to change or combat the myths that television fosters?

Not as much as they wish, perhaps, but it *is* possible to counteract some of the worst effects of sex stereotyping on TV. A few suggestions follow.

1. Keep the problem in perspective. Television is a strong influence, but it does not overwhelm the effect of a home where adults themselves work to overcome stereotypes in their daily lives. One father who stays home to care for a sick child, one mother who puts up the storm windows, one family friend who talks about her work with zest, siblings of either sex who help to cook and to clean up — these everyday influences are crucial. Adults whose own consciousness about sex role is raised are realer, more salient models for children than the tiny, farcical images on a television screen.

2. Use other media to encourage a positive, feminist outlook. Fine books with non-sexist situations and strong, active characters of both sexes are constantly being published. Good biographies of competent, successful women are increasingly available. For children who like to read, books offer models of behavior and suggest the variety of role options available to children, teen-agers and adults today. Many people never outgrow their pleasure in reading aloud: try it. Eager and reluctant readers alike enjoy having books read to them. Too often this opportunity is overlooked as children learn to read.

Many librarians read aloud a portion of a book to "motivate" children to read further themselves. When a parent reads to a child there is the opportunity to stimulate critical thinking about the story. (For a list of non-sexist books for young readers, see the listing for "Little Miss Muffet Fights Back" in "Other Resources" in the Appendix).

Newspaper articles about prominent women or changing lifestyles are more common every day. Most older children find Ms. Magazine fascinating reading. Toys, learning materials, posters that foster new attitudes are available to parents and teachers. (See listing for Women's Action Alliance in the list of organizations in the Appendix).

3. Don't keep quiet when television blares out its stereotypes. Watching the shows your children watch is the best way to find out for yourself what messages television is sending them; making those messages explicit and discussing them with your children after the show makes your disagreement clear. Your opinion counts! (Many children find adult interruptions during programs intolerable, but like to talk about what they've seen when the show is over).

4. Teach your children to be critics. You cannot (and probably don't want to) watch every program your children will see. Help them to learn to separate myth and distortion from reality on television. Encourage them to analyze plots and criticize characterization. Teach them to understand the function of advertisements, and to question what the advertisements say.

5. Be aware of television program schedules and encourage your children to become selective and to watch shows about which they have read or heard encouraging reports. One program like Miss Goodall and the Apes, The Life of Miss Jane Pitman, or Free to Be You and Me carries more punch, because of its high quality, than dozens of mass-produced half-hour episodes. If you like to watch documentaries about real people, encourage your children to look at them along with you. The reality of documentaries is a fine antidote to the banality of much television fiction.

6. Don't underestimate your power over the networks. A small amount of mail has a disproportionately strong effect on

television executives' attitudes. Be clear about your purpose in writing; it should not be to ask for the censorship of programs you consider bad, but to point out what it is in those programs that you find offensive, and why. Letters of appreciation for positive programs have a powerful impact, also. Encourage others who agree with your position to write letters along with you.

The networks are powerful, but so is the public. Because of feminist pressure, new women characters have been added to Sesame Street. The National Association of Broadcasters has reduced the amount of commercial minutes that children see on Saturday and Sunday children's programs from sixteen minutes to twelve minutes an hour because of pressure from ACT, an advocacy organization begun by a few parents and teachers in 1968 that now speaks for thousands of supporters across the country (see Appendix for listing of ACT). Other ACT accomplishments include the Federal Communications Commission's policy statement that all television stations must provide a reasonable amount of programming for children, and that a significant part of it should be educational; the elimination of vitamin advertising by the three largest drug companies in the country from children's shows; and the appointment of vice-presidents in charge of children's programming on many stations. In the fall of 1974, a chain of public television stations in the South was denied an FCC charter renewal because of racist hiring policies and all-white programming, after data from volunteer monitors was presented as evidence.

People do have power: the power to complain, to praise, to pressure — most of all, the power to teach children to be critical of all stereotypes, and to demonstrate through their own lives the values of equality for all people.

Part Two

THE TELEVISION PROGRAMS

This section of the report consists of brief plot summaries from one episode of each of the series viewed. They are arranged here according to the nights they were aired during the 1973 and 1974 seasons. Thus, we have condensed the prime-time dramas of two seasons into a hypothetical week's viewing.

In general, the plot summaries reveal two basic styles of writing: the farcical (Mash) and the uplifting (The Waltons). In the first, programs are based on misunderstandings, zany gags, crazy characters — and the jokes are underlined by laugh tracks that seem to approach hysteria. In the uplift programs good triumphs over bad, men save women and violence is justified by circumstance. There are no laugh tracks on these programs.

Each episode summarized here was selected arbitrarily from reports of three episodes per program viewed. (While the summaries skim over the dialogue and omit some scenes, the overall flow of each episode is reported). (A sampling of commercials is included). The episode of Maude dealing with the Equal Rights Amendment was chosen because of the relevance of its topic to the concerns of this report. Over and above the exaggerations of the plots, there is a recurring attitude of deprecation toward women. Women are treated as sexual objects (Mash, Temperature's Rising, Sanford and Son), ordered about by males (All in the Family, Lotsa Luck), permitted to serve men while being set on pedestals (The Waltons, The

Little House on the Prairie) and shown in stereotypically house-wifely roles (The Brady Bunch, The Girl with Something Extra). In Cannon, Hawaii Five-O, Kung Fu and Adam-12, women are victims, rescued by men. Even in shows where women have verve and character (Adam's Rib, Maude, Mary Tyler Moore) jokes are made about their situations and personalities. In the 1973 shows, perhaps only Diana was shown as independent and equal to a man, and even here (or *there*, since the program is no longer on the air) the emphasis is on Diana's relationships rather than on her career.

Rhoda breezed onto television as the star of her own show in the fall of 1974, and immediately captured the ratings. A spin-off from the Mary Tyler Moore show, Rhoda is something special: a vigorous, warm, witty woman who likes her work and loves her husband. Unfortunately, Rhoda's marriage has spawned more newlywed clichés than new ways. But Rhoda seems to be trying to be a new woman.

However, in most of the programs viewed, women and girls — and, it should be added, very often men — behave in ways that are at best stereotypically narrow, and at worst, as in the travesty of middle-age represented by Edith Bunker, ridiculous and demeaning.

LOTSA LUCK

Stanley works in the Lost and Found Department of a bus company. He lives at home with his mother, shown as a stupid, manipulative housewife, his sister Olive whose hair is constantly in curlers, and his brother-in-law who wears his bathrobe all day and does no work at all. Stanley is the breadwinner and the "decision maker." The program was taken out of production in the spring of 1974.

November 12, 1973. Stanley is looking for a date. He goes through his little black book looking for "girls" he can call up.

Mom: What kind of girl can you telephone on such short notice?

Arthur: The girls Stanley goes out with, he don't need no telephone. All he needs is a dog whistle.

Mom: Why must it always be *young* ladies?

Stanley: Are you kidding? Do you know what someone my age looks like when it's a girl?

Stanley's friend Bummy says Stanley needs a new suit; then they can go to the singles bar which is filled with gorgeous women. "You got to beat them off with a stick." Stanley borrows $25.

Later, he is dressed in his new suit. He and Bummy enter the singles bar. "You take the blond. I'll take the brunette."

Blond: You old guys slay me. Why don't you put on your ring and go home to your wife?

Bummy discusses his ways of luring women to his apartment. He has a color TV, a stereo, psychedelic lights. "If you want birds to fly in, you've gotta leave some crumbs on the window sill."

Stanley sits with another woman, boring her. A man comes over and kisses the woman; she asks him, "What did you say your name is?"

Stanley says maybe he should get a hair piece. He gets a styling as well.

At home, Arthur, Mom and Olive are playing cards. Arthur gets up. Olive asks where he's going.

"To get a beer."

"Why don't you ask me what I want?"

"What do you want?"

"A cream soda."

"Well, then, you can get me a beer."

But Arthur ends up getting the drinks.

Stanley comes downstairs in his hair piece. Olive and Mom supportively say he looks good, but Arthur doubles over in hysterical laughter.

At the singles bar, an old-timer rants on about young people today, and picks a fight with Stanley, whom he mistakes for a long-haired hippie.

The woman Stanley is with says, "Are you going to let him talk to you like that?" (She expects him to fight).

Stanley takes off the wig. He doesn't want to fight. "I'm bald but I'm still alive."

In this program, nobody seems to win. Stanley's attitude toward women is crudely sexist, but he himself is a victim of the singles bar and the desperate effort to appear young, attractive and manly.

DIANA

This show, one of the few programs that showed people relating to each other honestly and warmly, was taken off the air in spring of 1974. Diana, the main character, is an energetic, independent and resourceful young Englishwoman in New York. She is able to argue intelligently, has a sense of humor and generally projects a positive image. Although Diana works in a department store as a fashion designer, the program focuses on her relationships with men; the basic plot is the attempt of a young man to pursue Diana. In each episode, she retains her independence.

November 5, 1973. Diana's friend (Steven Green) is in her apartment watching the football game on television. She is reading the newspaper but comments, "American men have an unhealthy preoccupation with football. As a matter of fact, I'm beginning to think it's taking the place of sex."

Steven is drinking a Red Dog (beer). Diana asks why the drink is called that, and Steven replies that red is more masculine than cerise.

Steven goes over Diana's features with his fingers. (He is a plastic surgeon).

"Your nose is perfect — you have a Steven Green nose." But Diana answers that her lips are too thin, her nose is too full, and she has rabbity teeth.

Steven suggests going out. She gets the newspaper and reads off everything that's happening. He says, "No" to everything but finally agrees that cycling is a good idea.

Later, in a restaurant, they discuss a movie they've seen. Diana feels that the arguments and fights between the movie couple were stimulating and could end in bed. Steven feels that fights lead to divorce. If he had been the character in the movie, he would have walked out. He says he and his former wife fought all the time and ended up in divorce, not in bed. Diana persists. "When two people really care about each other and they get into a real knock-down drag-out fight all their real emotions and passions come out." In fact, she feels that this fight that they are having is stimulating. Steven agrees.

Meddling friends try to talk Diana into marrying Steven. "He'd make a good catch." "He's a successful doctor." "Nothing feeds an older man's ego like having a young beautiful wife." "He knew how to treat a woman the way an older man knew how to treat a woman. You know, with flowers, and dinner in the most expensive restaurants."

Diana responds to these statements by saying she needs time to think about it. Her friend exclaims, "No! Don't think about it too long. That was my mistake." Her man ran off with a 19-year-old stewardess.

In the next scene, Steven tells Diana, "I don't want to hurt you. I enjoy being free. Marriage for me would be very bad."

Diana asks, "Who said anything about marriage?"

Later, talking over her time with Steven, she says, "We had a wonderful week together. We're going to see each other from time to time with no strings attached."

Despite her obvious attractiveness, Diana is shown as insecure about her looks and dependent upon a man's approval. But this program also shows an unstereotyped relationship between Steve and Diana. They enjoy being together even though "no one said anything about marriage."

MAUDE

Maude is Archie Bunker's sister-in-law, and his opposite in many ways; she is a politically liberal, liberated woman. However, Maude's treatment on the show is consistently stereotypical. She is shown as manipulative, bossy, sarcastic, pushy, loud, aggressive, and emotional or hysterical as well. Thus, the program has it both ways: it presents, and demolishes, the stereotyped figure of a "liberated" woman. The joke, as with All in the Family, lies in the put-down of the main character — in this case, a straw woman. The script writers' feelings about women can be seen in the unbelievably crude theme song which refers to Joan of Arc who was a sister who really cooked and Isadora, the first bra burner.

November 27, 1973. Maude and Walter are to go to a dinner honoring Maude's work for the Equal Rights Amendment (a newspaper announcement refers to them as Mr. and Mrs. Walter Finley).

Arthur (a neighbor) compliments Walter. "Very clever of you to get in on this equal rights thing . . . what better way to get in with the ladies than to subscribe to this equal rights nonsense!"

He points out that, since Walter sells washing machines, it's good for Walter's business.

"I'm not saying the amendment's all bad. I believe in equal pay for equal jobs. I think female secretaries should get the same pay as male secretaries."

"What about equal pay for men and women executives?" asks Maude.

"Women shouldn't be executives. They're too emotional."

Maude: (in very emotional tone) Too emotional?

Arthur: See? Right away, you get emotional. Can you imagine what it would be like in this country if we had a woman president? Heaven help us if the hot line should ring at the wrong time of the month! . . . This Equal Rights Amendment strikes at the very heart of the American family. We'll end up with a country full of working mothers, neglected husbands, crying children, all because of women's lib."

Maude carries on about the Equal Rights Amendment — she is loud, assertive, combative and self-righteous. Meanwhile, she is strangling Walter as she ties his black tie, and others laugh at her as she continues her harrangue.

The cleaner comes with Maude's dress. "A bunch of nutty dames are dragging their poor husbands to some stupid thing for women's rights, ha, ha."

Maude's buttons will have to be sewn on. She is hysterical.

Arthur: Don't worry if you're a little late. They expect that of a woman.

Maude says Walter treats her like a human being.

Arthur talks about Grace's husband, who protected her after his death by appointing a trustee.

Walter confesses that he too has a trustee in his will — and it's Arthur. Maude is furious.

Walter: You don't know what it's like out there for widows.

Maude: Walter, allow me to make my own mistakes . . . trust me.

Walter: It's not a matter of trust, I do trust you . . .

Maude: Yes it is, Walter, and that's all it is. And I don't want to hear another word about it.

Walter: If that isn't just like a woman . . . A man knocks himself out trying to explain . . . Maude, I married you to take care of you, but not till just death do us part, either. Because I'm not letting my grieving, helpless, little old widow get taken by some greasy-haired gigolo.

Maude and Walter are arguing furiously. She puts on ear-muffs so she can't hear him.

Walter: Now you listen to me, Maude. I'm sick and tired of your attitude. If you want to wear the pants in the family, here — (he drops his trousers).

The committee to escort the Finleys to the dinner arrives in time to see this. Walter insists she accept the estate. He's panicky, she's yelling . . .

Walter: MAUDE — SIT!!

Maude: All right, Walter, you win, as usual.

Later, after the dinner, Maude is embarassed and angry over Walter's acceptance speech: "Thanks for making me the husband of the year. With my wife, it ain't easy."

And the Equal Rights Amendment has been turned into a cheap joke, thanks to a TV program about "women's liberation."

RHODA

Rhoda is Mary Tyler Moore's best friend, spun off into a show of her own. Married on its second episode, Rhoda copes with life as a newly-wed, work as a window-decorator, and the burdens of being her Jewish mother's daughter.

November 4, 1974. Rhoda and Joe are in bed; it's their wedding night and they're spending it, as they wanted to, at home.

Rhoda: I was just thinking back on all the nice things that happened — like an hour ago.

She and Joe agree that they don't feel different, though Rhoda says "for the first time in my life there's a stomach muscle that's relaxed."

Rhoda asks Joe if he wants her to fix his breakfast. Joe,

42

who is clearly very happy, says "No." "Hello, happiness," Rhoda responds. And then, "Do you realize there's one person who's happier? My mother." (She speaks fondly, though deprecatingly, of her mother throughout the episode).

Later, Rhoda visits her sister Brenda to discuss the wedding.

Brenda: Pop had a few drinks and asked everybody to guess what the wedding cost; Ma had a few drinks and she told them.

Rhoda's mother calls up to invite herself and Rhoda's father to dinner and give the newlyweds a wedding gift. Rhoda says the wedding was present enough, but her mother says that was a present to *her*. (She feels she has worked for many years to marry Rhoda off). Rhoda and Brenda make faces as Rhoda hangs up saying, "the champ."

At the apartment, Ida and Lou, the parents, arrive, with Ida asking whether there's been any news from the stork yet. Rhoda serves take-out chicken with aplomb.

Ida, about the wedding present: We've been waiting to do this for a long time. A *very* long time.

They've been putting away money for a wedding gift, and it's taken so long that the gift is a big one — tickets for a cruise. Rhoda and Joe are grateful, but restrained.

Ida, Lou, Rhoda and Joe, Rhoda's sister Brenda and Nick (the accordianist from the wedding party) are in the small cabin of the cruise boat. There is some uncomfortable joking, and a champagne toast, after which Rhoda and Joe are left alone.

At sea. Cruise members are dancing in the ballroom — all of them, except for Rhoda and Joe, senior citizens. The contrast between them and the young couple is played for laughs at the expense of the older people. Joe and Rhoda exchange partners with two of the old folks, and fall back to the table only to find an old man asleep there. A harried younger man arrives; he is the ship's doctor, overworked. The MC announces that there's a honeymoon couple aboard, and Joe and Rhoda reluctantly dance a waltz alone, in front of everyone ending up outside the ballroom.

In the next scene we see them at a bar on land. "Who would ever guess that the first stop on this cruise would be Baltimore?" Rhoda laughs. The boat whistle blows, the cruise party moves out, and Joe and Rhoda conspiratorially stay behind.

Throughout the episode, the love of Joe and Rhoda has been shown clearly and affectionately. Despite the stream of Jewish-mother jokes, Rhoda's happiness prevails. This is the real theme of the show.

"And now, a commercial break —"

*"He touched me, and suddenly nothing is the same."
—Chantilly*

"Tide was designed with mothers in mind." — Tide

Father and son racing on motorcycles, eating Wheaties. Male voice over: "He knows he's a man." — Wheaties

Woman at square dance, looking at man's shirt. "Ring around the collar!"

Woman with man winces; later she's seen scrubbing wildly. — Wisk

ADAM-12

The episodes follow two policemen in their daily rounds in the "Adam-12" patrol car. The policemen solve problems, save people, help young and old. They are shown as considerate, conscientious, brave, inventive, hard-working, clever and kind. The central characters in Adam-12 are all men. The only women in the three episodes viewed were treated as sex objects or as weak, drunken or crazy victims on whom the policemen practice their healing art.

November 21, 1973. The police car is cruising. The voice of a female radio operator is heard.

"Sounds like a new girl," says Pete.

"Say, she's all right." A moment later, he says, "I'd like to meet her." Jim quips, "C'mon, how many times have we been through this?"

The car is called to a hit-run accident. A little girl has been hurt. The police question her brother and get the car's license number. They arrange for a nurse to stay with the child until her mother comes. Fade out.

Back to a discussion of the operator. "I'd like to meet her."

The next call is about a burglary in a synagogue. The rabbi won't let them take fingerprints because it's Rosh Hashanah. The police are understanding. Fade out.

In the car, the men discuss the kind of person who could be a hit-and-run driver. They joke about getting time off. They discuss the radio operator and several former operators. One sounded as though she looked like Raquel Welch but she turned out to weigh 180 pounds.

Now there's a call about a drunk woman. She is sitting on the grass. The woman calls for her "baby daughter." The policemen drive her to her daughter's house. The daughter is a grown woman who rejects her mother because she had been trying to break up her marriage and asks the police to take her away. They do. Fade out.

Again the men fantasize about the radio operator, wondering what she looks like. Again they discuss the appearance of former operators. One had buck teeth. One was skinny.

They take a lunch break, and the ex-convict who runs the lunch wagon tells them that a man stopped in and threatened to shoot his former boss. The operator's voice is heard. More discussion of the "new girl." The lunch wagon operator says that voice is driving everyone crazy.

The car is sent to the scene of a shoot-out, where other cars and police join in an attempt to rescue a wounded man. They are careful, thoughtful and efficient. The man surrenders.

The final scene is at the police station. A woman approaches and introduces herself to the policemen: she's the radio operator. Immediately they offer to take her for a ride in the patrol car . . . "to see what it's like." She already knows. Her husband, who now approaches, is Lieutenant Edwards. Off they go and the policemen are left to their fantasies.

The whole episode is loosely hung on the patrolmen's interest in the radio operator as sex object — not as an intelligent, useful member of the police team.

HAWAII FIVE-O

Hawaii Five-O is essentially a male adventure show, about detectives — good guys — who are shown with a wide range of positive traits: they are competent, efficient, assertive, rational, and problem-solving. They are also violent. Violence is an integral part of the show, and the heroes do not question it. In many episodes, there are no women with speaking parts.

November 27, 1973. A big package called a "freezer" is delivered to the "commissary." It ticks.

The governor reads a threatening note in his limosine. An A-bomb will level Honolulu unless $100 million in blackmail is paid. The governor goes to see Dr. Haig, a nuclear expert at the University.

After the governor has left, Dr. Haig makes a phone call: "The pigeon is in the coop." It is clear that he is one of the criminals.

It is revealed that a Swiss metallurgist had died of radiation poisoning, and that the hospital had covered this up; now exhumation reveals the cause of death. Because the Swiss was a resident alien, detectives find where he worked — the refrigeration company — and burst into the building, but it's empty. However, their Geiger counter registers radiation. There are only eight hours left in which to find and de-fuse the bomb.

The Governor, the detectives, government and military officials — and Dr. Haig — meet to discuss the situation. They've raised the blackmail money. The criminal boss, "Mercury," calls with instructions for the delivery of the money. To prove his seriousness, he says there will be a "radiation flash" in the park that afternoon.

Police evacuate the park. Meanwhile, the detectives go to

Dr. Haig's house to get a detector. Haig goes inside alone, tries desperately but unsuccessfully to make a phone call, mumbling that he won't be a party to murder. A detective follows him inside and takes a page of doodling off one of Dr. Haig's note pads.

At the park, a radiation device is found in an ice cream vendor's cart. Dr. Haig insists that he will dismantle it, and does; the device explodes in a rest room. Haig is exposed to radiation.

The detective finds that Haig's doodle is the symbol for mercury. Dr. Haig feels so guilty that he makes a recording about his involvement, telling how he was tricked into it. He is weak from radiation exposure. He loads a gun but collapses before he can shoot himself.

The detective enters. Dr. Haig tells him where to search for the bomb and the detective says that Haig must hang on so he can dismantle the bomb when it is found.

The bomb is found. Haig supervises the dismantling. It is precise and dangerous work.

Meanwhile, at the airport, there is a police stakeout. A car loaded with money is driven down the runway by a detective. A plane lands. Oriental men get off the plane, load money from the cart onto it, and the plane begins to taxi away.

Back at the de-fusing scene, a detective radios to the airport: the bomb has been de-activated.

Police sharpshooters at the airport shoot at the escaping plane, and it bursts into flames.

A detective tells Haig that the men have been stopped. Haig tells the detective that mercury is an evil concept. Then

Haig is taken off in an ambulance, presumably to die.

Once again, the male detectives have accomplished their dangerous, clever work, in a world largely unpopulated by females.

TEMPERATURE'S RISING

This show is essentially a one-joke plot based on the doctor-patient relationship. Doctor Mercy is shown as a silly, sometimes paranoid head of a hospital. His receptionist is over-protective, devoted and inept. Dr. Claver generally portrays the manly physician. The patients are victims. The program was taken out of production in spring, 1974.

November 20, 1973. Dr. Mercy and his receptionist, Tillis, decide to leave the hospital ward to go for coffee.

A patient buzzes for help, complaining about an imagined illness. The nurse calls an intern, who decides the problem is appendicitis. The patient complains that this is only an intern's diagnosis, and climbs onto a window ledge, already convinced he's incurable.

Dr. Mercy sees the patient on the ledge and runs to the room where the intern is trying to persuade the patient inside. "Sometimes sex works," Mercy says, and the nurse obligingly sticks her head out the window.

Dr. Claver, drunkenly returned from his nephew's wedding, uses "psychology" and grabs at the patient, who falls (a few feet) to the ground.

Claver looks the patient over and decides to operate. Mercy and intern discuss the situation; Mercy won't forbid the operation, but when he walks in on Claver throwing up into the sink, he changes his mind. Claver storms out and the intern operates.

Tillis finds Claver asleep in the maternity ward. Sobered, he goes to apologize to Mercy. Now *Mercy* is drunk. Later, sobered, he apologizes to everyone. The final shot is of an intern who rushes into a closet and begins to kiss a nurse. A new day has begun.

Sexism is a staple part of this program's farcical treatment of hospital life. No matter how foolishly male doctors behave, they always get to give the orders and kiss the nurses.

THE LITTLE HOUSE ON THE PRAIRIE

Based on the much-loved "Little House" books by Laura Ingalls Wilder, this series is a natural for family viewing. However, the relationship of the parents to each other and to their three small daughters, so traditional and strong in the books, becomes tritely stereotypical in the television episodes. And the small details of pioneer life which make the books real are often lost in the fast-moving TV adaptation.

November 6, 1974. Ma is serving dinner to the family. When she sits down herself, Pa says he must deliver some lumber to town, and that he's arranged for a neighbor to come and stay so that Ma can go too. She says she can't possibly leave the children, but they urge her to go.

The woman turns out to be too sick to come. The girls beg to have Mr. Edwards, another neighbor, for a babysitter. Ma is apprehensive, but Pa and the girls convince her that Mr. Edwards will be fine.

Ma: I'm sure Mr. Edwards has things he'd rather do than take care of three little girls. Now if they were boys . . .

Laura: We can do anything boys can do.

Pa: I'll feel a lot safer having a man around while we're gone.

Mr. Edwards has come and is telling the girls tall tales. The baby plays with dinner. What if Ma could see?

Mr. Edwards: Nobody is going to tell Ma, is they? He gives the baby's uneaten food to the dog, and goes out to do the "man's job" — feeding cows and cleaning the stalls.

Meanwhile, Ma and Pa are in sleeping bags by a campfire. Ma remembers she forgot to remind the girls to gather the eggs. Pa says he'll buy her a bonnet if she'll stop talking about the girls for the rest of the trip. He says they used to have lots to talk about before the girls were born. Ma promises not to spoil this second honeymoon by worrying, but she continues to worry.

Back home, the baby is crying. Mr. Edwards gets out of bed and fixes her dinner, but she goes back to sleep before he has finished. He gives the dinner to the dog. In the morning the older girls are late for school because Mr. Edwards forgot to wake them. It is clear that Mr. Edwards is a bumbling, but good-hearted, baby-sitter.

Ma and Pa are eating in a restaurant. When Pa agrees that the food is good, Ma tells him that he was supposed to say it wasn't as good as her cooking. She worries about the cost of the meal. She says she's not worrying about the girls, but a minute later she's pointing out that at least they won't go hungry.

At home, Mr. Edwards is sleeping through a thunderstorm that wakes the girls. They remember they were supposed to gather eggs, and go out to do it. The chickens wake and cluck, and Mr. Edwards wakes up and grabs his gun to shoot the chicken thieves. The girls run in and the gun goes off, blowing a hole in the roof. Mr. Edwards sets out a bucket to catch the rain.

Ma and Pa are in a hat store. A woman wanders in and asks for her children; the storekeeper later tells Ma that the poor woman's children died 15 years ago in an electrical storm when the mother was away and that she hasn't been well since. Ma, upset, leaves without the bonnet. Later, she and Pa go to the theater, where the play is "Abandoned Daughters." The actress says she must leave her children for her own life. Ma cries and she and Pa leave in the middle.

At home, Mr. Edwards is fixing the roof. He and the girls decide they won't tell Ma and Pa about it unless they ask.

Ma and Pa are driving back home. Ma apologizes and says that it wasn't much of a second honeymoon for Pa, with her worrying. Pa is sorry she didn't get her bonnet.

At the house, they're squabbling over who will do the chores.

One of the girls goes to the store with the eggs and sees Ma and Pa coming. She rushed home and everyone cleans frantically. Ma and Pa arrive with gifts and see nothing awry.

Pa (to Mr. Edwards): You know how women are, if they're not around every minute, they think the roof will cave in . . .

How women are (always worrying and upset) and how men are (incompetent around the home) has been well demonstrated by Ma and Mr. Edwards. Pa, meanwhile, has taken charge and managed things.

Only the girls' hard work and verve reminds us of the strong, competent behavior of female as well as male pioneers.

"And now, a commercial break —"

Male voice-over picture of woman: "She's not inno- cent, not ordinary any more." — Revlon Color Silk

A woman speaks: "Every time I clean my bathroom bowl . . ." — Vanish

Woman in short skirt, jumping up toward mailman: "They fit! They really fit! My panty hose fit!" —Active

Woman flings her shining hair: "To know you're the best you can be . . ." —Clairol

---

THE GIRL WITH SOMETHING EXTRA

"Something Extra" is the Extra-Sensory Perception of the program's central character, Sally, whose amazing ability is put to fairly mundane problem-solving, like working out family difficulties or solving troubles with the law. As in situation comedies that must muddle along with characters whose perceptions are only adequate, the plots in "Something Extra" hinge on misunderstood intention, and the E.S.P. is little more than a gimmick to move them along. The program was taken out of production in the spring of 1974.

December 7, 1973. Sally is going to meet her new husband John's mother for the first time. She is anxious about her appearance as well as the possible effects of her E.S.P.

John's mother greets the couple exuberantly, and Sally finds her E.S.P. is working; she perceives that John's mother in fact hates her. While the mother compliments Sally on the decor of the apartment, Sally knows that she *really* thinks it looks like a "hippie church." The mother insists she knows just how John likes his tea, but Sally is aware this isn't true. The mother presents her favorite vase as a housewarming gift.

John's brother tells his mother that John is lucky to have married a girl like Sally, and then compliments his mother on her youthfulness: "I never called you Mother because you never looked old enough to *be* a mother." When Sally says, "Good night, Mom," the retort is, "You can call me Betsy."

To win her mother-in-law over, Sally decides to read her mind, find out what would please her and provide it. In bed, John tries to initiate sex, but Sally rebuffs him: "Your mother's downstairs."

Sally prepares what she secretly learns is Betsy's favorite meal — roast duck, with a sauce made from an old family recipe.

John: Now you know why I married her — because she cooks just like you.

But Betsy finds out that Sally has been reading her mind, and decides to leave. John, Sally and John's brother all apologize for duping Betsy. Sally overdoes the apologies. She returns the gift vase.

Eventually, Betsy, John, Sally and John's brother get together and Betsy forgives them all. Sally repairs the engine in her car. Betsy and Sally apologize and explain their misperceptions, talking honestly to each other at last.

Despite such novelties as E.S.P. and a woman repairing her car, the program's plot hinges on the old stereotyped mother-in-law joke, with women's concern over cooking, interior decoration and the proprieties of life thrown in. "Something Extra" — but nothing really new.

CANNON

Cannon is a fat detective who works out of a television series full of complicated plots and wordless action: running, driving, flying and walking down dark streets in pursuit of crooks, pimps, Mafiosi and unscrupulous businessmen. On many episodes a female guest is introduced only in order to be mistreated and rescued. Usually she appears at the beginning of the episode, disappears during the main actions, then reappears for the finale. These women are of two types: jaded women of experience, or naive, childlike girls. To all women, Cannon is paternal; he pats their cheeks, and flatters them in return for favors or information. For the same information, Cannon passes out $20 bills to men.

February 13, 1974. "I'll wait lunch," says Jill, as her husband, veterinarian Malcolm, leaves to give a tranquilizing shot to a lion in the animal park. Alas, lunch goes uneaten; the lion kills Malcolm.

Jill is playing the piano when Cannon appears with the news. "It's good therapy," she says, "for a scared little girl with braces, against mean teachers and even meaner little boys."

Jill thinks her husband must have been murdered. At the scene of the death, Cannon is told that Malcolm had some trouble with a Bantu helper who might have been the killer.

Cannon tries a lead: "Did Malcolm have a girl stashed away somewhere?"

He goes to the lab, where a former girlfriend tells him, "Whatever you want, the answer is No."

Cannon: "Now honey, that's no way to talk to a tired old lover, is it?"

She gives in easily, makes the test for him, and finds traces of energizer in the tranquilizer hypodermic.

A policeman shows Jill films of the death scene that have been sent in as evidence. "Cannon says I shouldn't have let you see that," says the policeman, protectively.

In Jill's living room, Cannon asks about the Bantu and about another woman in her husband's life, "Hilda."

Jill becomes hysterical.

"That woman has nothing to do with the murder." It develops that Malcolm and Hilda once went on safari together.

"I drove him to it, it was my fault. . . ."

On the way to the travel agency to get Hilda's address from the safari list, Cannon is almost bitten by a snake in his car. He finds Hilda at the hospital where she works as a nurse.

"Did she send you? That brave little widow, Jill Lawrence?"

Cannon interviews the Bantu, Anjara, and the park supervisor, who tries to make Cannon think Anjara killed Malcolm. Cannon is clearly suspicious of the supervisor.

Now some action shots: a sniper on the roof shoots at Cannon. The supervisor runs off. Cannon finds a Rhino rifle.

Cannon studies an aerial view of the park with Jill. He asks about shipment of animals and their cages.

Jill is confused and of no help. "I'm no expert," she shrugs.

The supervisor's assistant has been killed with a Rhino gun. Anjara is accused again, but Cannon believes he's innocent. Anjara is arrested. "What will happen to my wife?" he pleads.

Cannon reassured him. "I give you my word she will be taken care of."

Secretly, Cannon watches cages being unloaded at the animal park. The superintendent tranquilizes a lion, get him out of his cage, — and then takes heroin from the floor of the cage. The lion recovers and turns on the superintendent, and Cannon saves him.

"I just saved you so I could put you in jail."

Anjara is freed. Jill will take over the running of the animal park.

"I just hope it won't be too much for me. . . ." she says tentatively.

Small joke: Anjara offers Cannon a ride on an elephant.

"I couldn't do that to an elephant," Cannon responds.

Both racism and sexism are evident in the paternalistic

treatment of "the Bantu" and women on this episode. The women shown exhibit deference to men, hysteria, jealousy and insecurity. Cannon, on the other hand, is brave, attractive, and clever.

THE WALTONS

Childhood in the depression. John-Boy, the central figure, shares a warm family life with parents, brothers and sisters and grandparents. The atmosphere is loving and supportive; hard times seem to be surmountable by force of character. Most plots focus on John-Boy's experiences as he grows toward manhood. It is John who seems to grow in the series; the girls are more often involved in trivial sub-plots, and the adult women service the family's needs and echo their men's opinions. They stay in the background while the men fix, build and solve problems.

November 8, 1973. Erin, a sister, is in the schoolyard giving a hand-sewn handkerchief to a boy, when another boy yanks it away and makes fun of the gift.

At dinner John-Boy talks about a rent collecting job in which he's interested.

Erin mopes about "dumb old Harold Beasley." The family goes berry-picking, and there, under a tree, is Harold Beasley. Erin's sister tells her not to notice him.

John-Boy gets the rent collecting job from the landlord, who is seen as unscrupulous by the Walton men. Apparently something happened in the past that left bad feelings between them. John-Boy accepts the job despite warnings from his elders and is determined to succeed.

Erin finds a fawn, separated from its mother. "I'll take care of you," she says.

The family discusses names for the fawn. Grandpa disapproves of keeping it. "When you go against nature, you're in a mess of trouble." Mother agrees. The kids go to bed, but Erin sleeps in the barn with her fawn.

John's first attempt at rent collecting: the man has no job and congratulates John on his. But when he finds that John's work is to collect his rent, he confesses he can't pay it all. John-Boy is polite, respectful, sympathetic.

The fawn pulls laundry off the line. The mother and grandmother are upset.

An old woman from whom John is collecting rent tells him that her roof is leaking, and that the landlord hasn't fixed it. John says he'll report it. She says, "You *are* young."

In the kitchen, Erin worries that the warden will take her deer away. The warden says, "It's the law; you can't keep her."

"Wait till my Daddy comes home."

Grandpa: It's the law, Erin, and nobody can interfere.

John is home, depressed about his work. He hates to quit because he feels he is a spokesman for the tenants.

Erin is in the barn with her mother. She says that the deer needs someone to care for it. Mother points out that Erin's need for the deer is greater than its for her. The other children are sympathetic to Erin.

John tells the landlord about the tenants' problems. The landlord is unsympathetic. John has come to get his pay, but the landlord refuses it, almost gloating. "You'll end up like your father."

Erin grieves for the deer. Her grandmother says, "Feeling sorry for yourself is a waste of time." The warden comes for the deer. Erin's mother apologizes, "She's just like a little girl." (Erin is 14).

John discusses the landlord with his father. "I made a fool out of myself," John says. The father offers to intercede, but John says No.

Erin has a nightmare about the deer. She runs to her parents' bedroom, and says to her mother, "Sometimes *you* have feelings about the people you care for, and don't you have to do something about these feelings?"

Two men are hunting the fawn. Erin and her father ring a bell to call it home. The hunters shoot and hurt the fawn, and the warden catches them. He arranges a solution: the fawn can go to an animal park, where Erin will be able to visit.

John confronts the landlord and quits his job. He manages to collect the rent, fix the broken roof and pay himself and the landlord. The landlord wants to re-hire him, but John refuses. In the kitchen, he talks to his father about the landlord, while his grandmother serves dinner. She says, "You should write a story about your sister and the deer."

In the barnyard, the family assembles to see the deer off to the animal farm. But Erin decides to let it go free, "because it's best for it." The deer hesitates, then bounds away.

John recalls, "My sister gave the deer its freedom, and decided to give boys another chance."

This episode, like many in the series, propounds home truths of unobjectionable morality. Stereotypical assumptions of how boys and girls grow up (the boys to school or work, the girls to marriage) underlie the plots, as they underlay the thinking of many real-life families, not too different from the Waltons, in the depression years.

KUNG FU

The male lead of Kung Fu is no ordinary man, but a former Buddhist priest who recalls his heritage in gong-clanging flashbacks of simplistic religiosity. Because he is a Buddhist, Caine is gentle, tender, supportive. Because he is a male in an American western, he is also a fighter of amazing dexterity and strength. Caine is a good guy, whose mission on each episode is to rescue someone who is being victimized by bad guys. Often, this person is a woman, physically weak and morally unenlightened, who falls over Caine in gratitude and looks wistfully after him as he walks away from her toward the next adventure.

December 13, 1973. Caine wakes up by a tree, with a flock of sheep in the background. A passing woman, holding a sick lamb, is thrown off her horse into a stream. Caine takes the woman back to her camp, a Hutterite colony, where Gretchen's father invites Caine to stay and do her work until her arm, broken in the fall, has mended.

It develops that cowboys are trying to stop the Hutterites from watering their animals in the stream. They believe the Hutterite animals have a contagious sickness. The sheriff warns the cattlemen to leave the Hutterites alone, but instead they shoot holes in the water barrels the Hutterites have filled to take to their sheep.

"Is there no place we can behave just as we choose?" asks Gretchen, as her father says they must move on. He will go to town, get a new wagon wheel, and explain to the sheriff that the sheep, though sick, are not contagious. But on his way to town he is stopped by the cattlemen, who shave his beard. The sheriff fines the cattlemen, and tells Caine and Gretchen's father that the Hutterites may bring their sheep to water every day at noon.

But the group decides to leave the camp ground. Gretchen is saddened. "Are we the ones who are wrong?"

A cattleman hovers over his dead cow, blaming the death on the Hutterites.

Gretchen's father talks about life with Caine, while a little boy hides in a box because he doesn't want to leave. Caine warmly teases him out of the box.

The cattlemen come to kill the Hutterites' sheep and burn their wagons. Excited women scream. Caine saves the day

in a battle with the cattlemen, who outnumber him ten to one. The sheriff appears and sends the cattlemen home.

Gretchen's father says they will stay even though the rest of the group leaves. Caine has made Gretchen a flute. Throughout he has been a kind spokesman of the world outside the Hutterite colony, proving to Gretchen that the world is not only full of wicked people like the cattlemen.

Caine's religious faith, his wish for non-violence, his gentleness to women and children are far from stereotypical. But he maintains an aura of invincibility and superiority far above that of the minor women characters who, like Gretchen of this episode, turn to him for guidance, clarification and protection. Caine may admire and respect them, but he is shown as clearly superior to such ineffectual women.

──────── *"And now, a commercial break —"* ────────

"There's a kind of warmth that's uniquely a woman's."
— Correctol

Woman: "I go through the motions of being hard to get!" — Nice and Easy

Woman: "I'll be the Me you can't resist!" — Rive Gauche

"I know where my wife learned all that good cooking — perfect mother-in-law, perfect rice!" — Minute Rice

---

SANFORD AND SON

Sanford and his son Lamont are black junkyard dealers. Most of the show's humor derives from role reversal: Sanford is childish, scheming, manipulative and almost senile. Lamont runs things. Women are minor characters, primarily presented as sex objects.

November 2, 1973. Sanford is suspicious of the well-dressed stranger who comes to the door, and doesn't want to identify himself. Lamont reproaches him, and the stranger turns out to be an insurance broker who announces that Sanford has inherited $1500 from a distant uncle in St. Louis.

Lamont makes arrangements for his father to fly to St. Louis, over the protests of Sanford, who is afraid to fly. Sanford gives in when Lamont reminds him of the commercial: "I'm Jackie, fly me."

At the airport, Sanford is afraid of the security check. Then he propositions the stewardess. After berating a huge man for smoking, he turns his anger on another, smaller man. He's afraid of the oxygen mask, afraid of the take-off, ignorant of airplane routine. He leers at the stewardess's behind. Lamont reproaches his father for this behavior.

At the lawyer's office, it becomes clear that the $1500 is only to pay for the uncle's burial. Sanford condemns the dead uncle in an angry, cynical manner. On the flight home, he makes faces at the unattractive stewardess.

Sanford has been shown as a *foolish* sexist, but the sexist stereotypes of the episode linger: a stewardess is to flirt with if she's attractive, to reject if she's not.

THE BRADY BUNCH

In a script writer's tour-de-force, the blond mother of three blond girls marries the dark-haired father of three dark-haired boys. Except for its make-up, and the presence of Alice, the household help, the family is fairly conventional. Plots hinge on misunderstandings not likely to occur in real life to normally sensible children and adults. The program was taken out of production in the summer of 1974.

December 7, 1973. Two of the girls hear Alice discussing the coming elopement of her boyfriend Sam's cousin, and become fixed on the idea that it is Alice and Sam themselves who intend to elope.

Everyone in the family is sure that Alice and Sam will elope; when Sam calls the father to find out how people go about eloping, he becomes certain. "If someone close to me were planning an elopement," he says, "they could trust me implicitly."

Alice asks for Saturday off. The family offers her the whole week, and reminds her to buy extra rice. Mother plans a reception for Alice, and begins interviewing replacements.

Alice and Sam argue about a wedding gift for Sam's cousin — should it be a bowling ball, or something more sentimental? They begin to fight, and break their date for Saturday night. Alice tells the family she won't need the night off after all, and they all try to talk her back into what they suppose is the elopement date.

Sam stops by with a conciliatory package of meat from his butcher shop: "Four extra lamb chops in pink panties." It's his way of telling Alice he's sorry. The Saturday date is back on.

"Take care of our girl, will you, Sam?" asks Father.

Alice and Sam return from their Saturday bowling date to a surprise wedding reception. Confusion and apologies. They make an announcement, not quite the one everyone hoped for: they've advanced to the finals of the bowling tournament.

After the cousin's wedding, they come home ecstatic, and engaged. But Sam says they've set only the date, not the century.

In this episode, Alice and Sam have confounded the paternalistic, sexist, foolish expectations of everyone around them by *not marrying* — a triumph for individuality on this traditionally stereotyped program.

CHICO AND THE MAN

Chico is a young Puerto Rican who works in an unprofitable auto repair shop owned by "the man" — Ed Brown, an older white person. A black trash collector named Louis is also a regular member of the cast. A warm sense of friendship among these three men is shown.

November 8, 1974. Chico is fixing a flat on a mini-bus. Ed asks why he's bothering to fix a flat on a vehicle that hasn't moved in four years. Chico explains that he *lives* in it, and that it doesn't feel so good to be in bed when a tire goes flat.

Chico asks for money for the interior decoration of the van. "I saw a picture of a rug in *House Beautiful* that I simply must have." Ed doesn't even have the money to pay Chico his wages.

Chico: "The main thing about working here is that when you go on unemployment, it's a step up!"

Ed says that he owes the bank $2,000. Chico suggests that he could pay this back by borrowing $3,000 from another bank, and still have $1,000 to use.

Ed describes his poverty in growing up. "I was so poor that the rich kids in my neighborhood were black."

Louis offers to loan Ed some money, because Ed has loaned him money in the past. Ed can't accept the offer because he feels he would never be able to pay it back.

An arrogant customer comes in for gas, asks what octane it is, and demands that his windshield be cleaned before Ed puts gas in. Ed throws a bucket of water at the windshield and tells the customer to leave before he gets charged for a car wash.

Chico again raises the possibility of another bank loan. But Ed goes into a humorous dialogue about how bad his credit is. "We could go to Break-A-Leg Kelly, but there's one problem. If you don't pay in time he takes your shoe, and by a strange coincidence your leg is in it."

Chico responds, "Man, you gotta have faith." He has just received a letter from Uncle Sam announcing that $2,000 is paid upon enlistment. This prompts Ed to tell the story of his "war wound", received outside a New Orleans brothel. He was shot in the backside by a ricocheting bullet and the lead is still in him. He had to leave the Signal Corps after the incident because they received enemy aircraft warnings every time he turned his back.

Chico does impressions of Marlon Brando, James Cagney and John Wayne as he convinced Ed to try to get a loan from the Veterans Administration.

Chico and Ed go to the VA to ask about loans. An interviewer asks them to establish their eligibility. He wants to know where Chico's parents were born.

Chico: "My father's Mexican, my mother's Puerto Rican and my grandmother speaks a little Hungarian."

Interviewer: "What does that make *you*?"

Ed: "An American."

The VA Administrator can't find Ed's records. He is upset because Ed has forgotten his Army serial number and hasn't kept his dog tags. When the administrator locates Ed's records, he asks if Ed was ever stationed in New Orleans. Chico says that's where Ed was wounded.

Administrator: "How did you get wounded in *New Orleans*?"

Ed: "I ran into a German patrol."

Chico and Ed learn they aren't eligible for a loan, but discover that the VA will pay students and instructors in accredited schools with veterans' programs. Chico persuades Ed to pretend they have an auto mechanics school in order to receive government payments. They involve Louis in their scheme, and set up a dummy school in Ed's garage. Chico designs a report card with subjects like Introduction to Greasing 101A and The Historical Significance of Maintenance.

Ed gets cold feet because the plan is dishonest, but Chico convinces him that his is entitled to some Army benefits.

A VA inspector arrives to observe the "school". Chico and Ed go through a charade of a lesson. The inspector is incensed and threatens to sue. Louis says, "Every time I try to go to school, trouble starts."

Most of the humor of this episode revolves around ethnic and racial joking. Ed's pessimism, and Chico's and Ed's attempts to manipulate and deceive the Veterans Administration into giving them a loan.

There is no sexism on this episode — but there are no women on it, either.

ADAM'S RIB

The only top-rated program of the 1973-4 season that seemed intended to be pro-feminist had vanished from prime-time by early spring of 1974. This is a pity, but some feminists, particularly those who don't mind being seen as "never satisfied," may not be too distressed that the saga of Amanda and Adam, a childless married couple in their thirties, both lawyers, is off the air. For although Amanda has a responsible position and a relatively independent business life, her personal relationship to Adam is more like that of a daughter than a wife. Adam is forever teaching Amanda a lesson, even going so far as leaving her in jail overnight in order to do so. In situation comedy-land, new gimmicks — "Let's show a working married couple!" — don't easily supersede old myths.

December 21, 1974. Amanda is in court, arguing a case before the judge. She enters a not-guilty plea for her client, although Adam has advised her to plead guilty. Later, in bed, they argue. Amanda bets $20 that any policeman would arrest a woman who initiates contact with a man in a public place as a prostitute, whether or not she mentions money. And the plot is ready to unfold.

Amanda learns the name of a bar where undercover agents look for prostitutes, and goes there. As she sits drinking alone, a former date appears.

"Where's Adam?"

The man seems unable to imagine that Amanda might have a drink alone in a bar.

When she sees a man in the bar alone, Amanda invites him to a show, and to go dancing. She has a tape recorder with her. The man identifies himself as a cop and takes her away as a soliciting prostitute.

Amanda is being tried in court for soliciting. She explains the situation. The judge accuses her of being mischievious. He fines her $500. Adam will not pay her bail, so she must spend the night in jail.

"It'll be good for you," says Adam.

After a sleepless night, Amanda is unable to conduct her own trial, but fortunately Adam rescues her with a brilliant defense.

Presumably, Amanda has learned her lesson in this episode: not to attempt to prove that inequality between men and women exists in initiating social contacts. And not to argue with her husband.

"And now, a commercial break —"

"My wife, she cares about herself, and I love her for
it." — Geritol

"A man-pleaser dinner you know will please your
man." — Man Pleaser Dinners

Woman serving obsequiously:
"Honorable husband have hamburger, hamburger
Japanese style." — Hamburger Helper

Woman, about her baby boy:
"If he's comfortable, I'm happy!" — Ivory Snow

ALL IN THE FAMILY

A program featuring Archie Bunker, the blue-collar head of
household who is more of a bigot than most people. Jokes
center around Archie's hates and his victims' discomforts.
Archie usually gets his come-uppance by the end of each
episode, and his bigotry is treated almost like a loveable foible.
Edith, wife and victim of Archie's petty tyranny, is essentially
a kind person who inevitably appears stupid and incompetent.
Carroll O'Connor, the actor who plays Archie, is quoted in
Good Housekeeping magazine:* "She wasn't exactly bright
at the beginning [of the series] but now she's approaching
a moronic level . . . . for myself, Carroll O'Connor, Edith is
an intolerable person."

November 10, 1973. Gloria, Archie's daughter, is cooking a
nutritious, economical dinner for the family — horsemeat.
She tricks her husband Michael into eating a bite. He runs to
the sink, yelling that he's eaten horse, but Gloria gets him to
admit that it really tasted good. She says she's planning not to
tell her parents.

Enter Irene, a neighbor, and her sister, Theresa, a nun.
Michael asks why Theresa is in street clothes, and Edith answers,
"Nowadays some nuns are allowed to go around just like they

---

*Good Housekeeping, 11/74, Interview: Mike Wallace with Carroll O'Connor.
 "Carroll O'Connor Answers the Tough Questions About 'Archie Bunker' "

was people."

Archie enters. He is rude to Theresa, and demands his dinner. He commands Edith, "Take the saint off ya," referring to a medal given to Edith by Theresa. "Why?" Edith implores.

"Because it's Catholic!"

After a serious explanation of the Catholic faith by Theresa, Archie responds with a put-down of the Pope.

Father Majerski is at the door. He and Archie exchange insults, then Archie turns on Gloria's dinner: "It must be either the Chink's or Colonel Saunders'."

Edith compliments Gloria on the dinner. Gloria whispers that it's horsemeat, and Edith leaves the table, hand over mouth, in horror.

Archie mocks Edith's recital of her day's interests and happenings. She leaves to pursue her interests with friends, to Archie's cry, "Edith, what are ya doing? You're running around like a loose weed."

Anxiety strikes Archie, and he visits Father Majerski to say that he fears Edith wants to convert. Father Majerski says Archie will have to talk to Edith himself. They trade insults.

Archie calls Edith stupid for going to church. He gets really angry, and waves his finger in front of Edith's nose: "You wouldn't even know what you done if you done it. Did you kiss anybody's ring tonight?" She asserts that she would never convert.

Irene defends her faith to Archie. She says the important thing is to love other people. Michael agrees. Archie insults Michael. Irene leaves, saying she's glad that the Protestants have Archie. Edith states her belief in one God. Archie: "Let me do the thinking. You just do the usual things around here like, for instance, get me a beer."

Edith complies: "Would you like a snack with it?"

Archie says he's hungry enough to eat a horse . . . . (Much laughter).

Thus, another evening of manipulative and derisive interaction at the Bunkers' closes. On this episode, religion has been mocked, a priest and several women have been belittled, and Archie has eaten horsemeat. The viewer is left to wonder whether Archie's punishment has been equal to his cruelty and bigotry. The question left hanging is whether Archie is really sort of a loveable bigot at heart. There is *no* question about Edith — as she has played the victimized fool.

M*A*S*H

Laughs in a front-line hospital, where war is presented as a game of wits. The two major characters are kind, competent, humorous army surgeons who won't conform to petty army routine. The antagonists are a female nurse and a male doctor who try to take control of the camp and run it according to regulations. There is a sexual relationship between this couple — the nurse is a sex-starved, dominating woman called Hot Lips Houlihan — and their general stance is one of righteous indignation. Other personnel: the commanding general, a bumbling non-conformist; Radar, his aide, usually incompetent and excessively concerned with eating; and the base nurses, who are ignored by everyone except at the cocktail hour.

November 3, 1973. It's Kentucky Derby Day at the post. Nurses are being pushed in a race in service wagons. There are cheers for "Bouncing Betty" and "Girl O'War".

Clinger is attempting to escape the army by flying off a small hill. Meanwhile, at a hearing, Blake is charged with "lack of firmness to command". The hearing is interrupted with reports on the escape attempt. "I think he might have made it if he had had a better tail wind."

Blake is placed under arrest and confined to quarters. Corp. O'Reilly is dispatched to get defense materials.

Outside, O'Reilly and other men discuss Blake's arrest. They believe it was engineered by Houlihan and Burns. They suggest helping Blake by bringing Nurse Cratty to the hearing next day.

Burns and Houlihan learn of the Nurse Cratty plan, and Burns places the men under arrest. How can they solve Blake's problems from their confinement?

"We're two captains against one major. If we were playing poker . . ."

"Let's not believe he's one of a kind."

"That's right. Hot Lips is a major too."

"That's a bigger pair!"

At the hearing Blake is charged with ordering extra medicine and supplies.

Blake admits sending these supplies to Nurse Cratty, who runs a clinic for South Koreans. He says the charges are substantially correct. His defense is that he was trying to help the clinic.

Enter Nurse Cratty with pregnant South Korean woman. She and dozens like her will have healthy babies, the nurse says, because Blake has supplied the clinic with medicines.

Burns and Houlihan accuse Blake's men of being AWOL, and stealing a jeep. The commander asks Houlihan and Burns to drop all charges. Burns refuses, on "patriotic grounds". The men pass him a note threatening to write his wife about the affair with Houlihan. They agree to withdraw charges.

Blake wishes Nurse Cratty good luck, and gets congratulations from all the men at camp.

The episode shows a strange mixture, typical for Mash, of social concern, farcical interaction, general hostility and arrogant sexism. Still Nurse Cratty emerges, along with Blake, as a decent person.

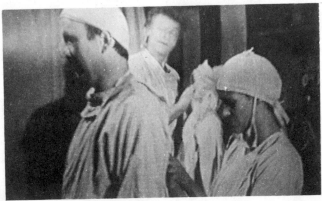

FRIENDS AND LOVERS

Something new for television: the story of a single man who plays bass for the Boston Symphony Orchestra. There is plenty of pressure on Robert to get married, but he resists — and has friendly, interesting relationships with women. The women on the show, however, appear generally insecure.

November 2, 1974. The musicians are backstage, talking about a coming dinner dance. Robert says he doesn't think he'll come. The manager firmly explains that "everybody comes".

Robert tells his friend Jack that he doesn't want to "scrape up a date" for the dance. His girl friends are away. One named Sandra has joined a religious commune. "No sex, only greens." Jack says, "Sounds like my marriage."

Robert and Jack are drinking at Robert's apartment. Robert talks about the pressure he feels not just to have a date, but a *terrific* date for the dinner dance. Jack says he takes the same girl each year. "Costs me fifty bucks but it's worth it. She's a real knockout."

At his brother's house, sister-in-law Janice tells Robert that she wants him to meet this great girl named Bambi.

Robert: Bambi. That's such a sweet name.

Charlie: Believe me, Robert, it's not the same Bambi.

But Robert is appreciative. He wants to meet Bambi first, and then perhaps he'll ask her to the dance.

In the rehearsal room, one of the musicians says he can get Robert a date with his cousin, Celia. Robert says he already has a date for tonight, and she'll be arriving any minute.

Celia enters. She's beautiful in a stereotypically "feminine" way. Robert says he's really sorry he's busy because he'd like to go out with her. She leaves, and Bambi (who is perfectly attractive) enters.

Bambi: "I'm sorry." (Apologetically.)

Robert asks why, and Bambi says that she just saw the beautiful woman he turned down. Robert says it's a pleasure to meet Bambi.

Bambi: Oh, that's terrific. The first thing I look for in a man is a sense of humor.

Bambi and Robert are entering a run-down bar where they've had to go because Robert's car has broken down. Robert calls the towing service. Someone will come for the car in "20 minutes to three hours." Robert suggests a game of pinball. Bambi says he'd better be a good loser, because she's going to cream him. They have a good time together, and when the repair man arrives Robert can't believe that three hours have passed. Meanwhile, Bambi has been full of defensive cracks about herself. When Robert goes for peanuts, she tells him that she once went to a movie with a guy who went for popcorn and never came back.

Robert is trying on his tux at Charlie's. Charlie apologizes for arranging the date with Bambi. Robert says he had a great time with her. Charlie asks who he's taking to the dance. Robert tells him about this beautiful girl, Celia.

Robert: I get the feeling that people judge guys by the girls they go out with.

He says looks aren't that important. In high school he took out a girl he liked whom everyone made fun of. But he isn't fifteen any more. "I don't have to make an impression on anyone." Charlie continues to press him to invite Celia to the dance.

Later, in the kitchen, Bambi and Janice are fixing supper. Bambi wonders how Robert will break the news to her that he doesn't want to take her to the dance.

The phone rings. It's Robert, asking for Bambi's phone number. He wants to ask her to the dance.

The final scene is in Robert's apartment. He's dressed for the dance, and Bambi enters. He's surprised; he was planning to go to *her* house. Bambi says that something often happens to a man and his car on the way to her house, and that's why she came to him.

Robert: You have nothing to worry about now. (He goes to the bedroom to get his jacket.)

Bambi: I'll go with you . . . (She follows him into the bedroom as though fearing he might escape.)

Throughout the episode, self-deprecating jokes are made by Bambi. Nevertheless, she is presented as clever and attractive. And Robert is shown as thoughtfully interested in working out his own ways of relating to women. It is surprising that so old a peg "as a date for the dance" holds a story of adults in 1975 together.

MARY TYLER MOORE

Mary is an appealing unmarried career woman in her thirties. She is Assistant Producer for a television station, but she is often shown performing secretarial duties like coffee-making, and more rarely seen in professional tasks. Mary is almost over-polite socially, and many incidents focus on her discomfort in awkward situations. She is presented as an insecure person, constantly seeking reassurance from her friends. Although she is shown to be happily single, there are references to her wish to be married.

November 2, 1974. Mary and Lou Grant are in Mary's apartment, working on ideas for a television documentary. Neither can come up with a good one. Mary cuts off her thoughts before she says them. Finally she suggests, "What about a documentary on women's changing roles?"

Lou: "That stinks."

Mary: "I know."

Phyllis, a neighbor, comes in wearing a new dress, fishing for compliments. "What I mean is, I am too plain to be a model — under any circumstances — whatsoever." Lou interrupts her. "We're working, Phyllis". Phyllis wants to borrow earrings to wear to the ballet with Mike, "the guy I go out with." She offers them the supernatural as a topic for a documentary. They thank her. Mary asks about Mike. Phyllis says that he's a companion of whom her husband approves.

Mike arrives and is introduced to Lou and Mary. As they leave, Phyllis says she knows her documentary idea is a good one; it was great when they did it on Channel Four.

Next day at the office Mary tells her colleagues Murray and Ted what a nice guy Mike is. Murray raises his eyebrows. He thinks Mike is a homosexual. Ted thinks it's disgusting that a married woman is going out behind her husband's back. Mary replies that Mike isn't interested in Phyllis for "that sort of thing."

Ted: "Oh, I get it, you mean the guy's a little . . ."

Mary: "Why do you assume that? I mean, the man is not. . ."

Ted: "Not what? You mean you and I aren't talking about the same thing?"

Mary: "Yes, we're talking about the same thing, and he's not."

Mike stops in. Mary introduces him and asks about the ballet. Ted thinks he was in it, rather than a spectator, but Lou explains.

Ted: "Either way, it's all right with me. I never care about a guy's race, religion or sex. Black or white, Jewish or gentile, A.M. or F.M."

Mike asks Mary to go out with him. She makes excuses: too busy, too much work. Says she'll call him. . .she's nervous.

At home, Mary brings ice cream to Phyllis, who has a cold. Mike arrives to take Phyllis to the opera, and Phyllis suggests he take Mary instead. Mary agrees.

At the office, Mary confides her concern to Lou: she's gone out five or six times with Mike and now she's beginning to feel a little funny because he's really Phyllis' friend. Lou asks how serious it is, and Mary says they're just friends.

Lou: "You mean he's never made a pass at you?"

Murray: "Maybe Ted was right about him."

Ted: "Do you seriously think a guy and a chick can go out five times together and nothing happens?"

Phyllis comes to Mary's apartment to return the earrings. Mary asks if Phyllis is upset because she's seeing Mike. Phyllis says that she's delighted. . .but does feel pangs of jealousy. She and Mary talk more frankly, and hug each other. Phyllis suggests they be really truthful and tell their ages. Mary says she's 34.

Phyllis: "Now I'm going to tell you my age for the first time and it isn't easy. I am 43 years old. That's right, Mary, 43. Aren't you going to say something?"

Mary: "Boy, are you old." (She explains she's kidding.)

Phyllis leaves and Mike arrives to break his date with Mary. He asks if she's wondered why he hasn't made a pass at her. Mary starts to say no but catches herself and says "Yes, as a matter of fact." Mike explains that when he began to see Phyllis he had just broken off with Sharon, the woman he had lived with for three years. Now they've made up, and are going to be married.

Phyllis comes in and Mike tells her about Sharon. Mike tells Mary that he thinks she's terrific. To Phyllis he says, "There are no words to describe you." He suggests that maybe someday they can all get together.

Mary: "Sure, some day Sharon, you, Phyllis and I can go dancing."

Phyllis and Mary talk supportively after Mike leaves. They hug.

The final scene: At the office, Lou suggests that open marriage might be a good idea for a documentary.

Murray objects: "I don't go for the idea of married people dating other people on a purely friendly basis."

Mary: "Come on, Murray, haven't you ever had a woman in your life who was a friend and companion without any physical contact?"

Murray: "Yes, my wife . . ."

New ideas jostle old stereotypes on this episode. Stock jokes about homosexuals, older women trying to appear attractive, and husbands bored with their wives are thrown about while Mary and Phyllis try quite sincerely to cope with new ways of relating to men — and to each other. Whether the viewer can hear new ideas over the banter is questionable.

Appendix

REFERENCES

1. Bandura, A. Social-learning Theory of Identifactory Processes, in Goslin, D., ed., *Handbook of Socialization Theory and Research.* Chicago: Rand McNally, 1969.

2. Barcus, F. Earle. Saturday Children's Television: *A Report of Television Programming and Advertising on Boston Commercial Television.* Prepared for Action of Children's Television, July, 1971, 54 pp. and appendix, available from ACT, $10.00.

3. Friedrich, L.K. and Stein, A.H. *Aggressive and Prosocial Television Programs and the Natural Behavior of Preschool Children.* Monograph of the Society for Research in Child Development. 38: 4, 1973.

4. Gerbner, G. Violence in Television Drama: Trends and Symbolic Functions, in Comstock, G.A. and Rubinstein, E.A., eds., *Television and Social Behavior,* Reports and Papers I: Media Content and Control. Washington, D.C.: U.S. Printing Office, 1972, pp.28 – 187.

5. Liebert, R.M., Neale, J.M., and Davidson, E.S. *The Early Window: Effects of Television on Children and Youth.* New York: Pergamon Press, 1973, p. 5.

6. Leifer, A.D. and Roberts, D.F. *Children's Responses to Television Violence.* Stanford, CA.: Institute for Communication Research, 1971.

7. Lyle, J. and Hoffman, H.R. Children's Use of Television and Other Media, in Rubinstein, E.A., Comstock, G.A., and Murray, J.P., eds., *Television and Social Behavior,* Reports and Papers IV: Television in Day-to-Day Life: Patterns of Use. Washington, D.C.,: U.S. Government Printing Office, 1972.

8. Nicholson, J., Hennessee, J., and Biele, D. Analysis of the Function and Roles of Males and Females in Television Advertising on WABC—TV April 24, 1971 – May 7, 1971. Manuscript prepared for the NOW New York City Chapter, 1972.

9. NOW National Capital Area Chapter, *Women in the Wasteland Fight Back: A Report on the Image of Women Portrayed in TV Programming.* Washington, D.C. 1973.

10. O'Connor, R.D. Modifications of social withdrawal through symbolic modeling in R.D. O'Leary and S.G. O'Leary (ed.) *Classroom Management.* New York, Pergamon Press, Inc. 1972.

11. Rosenkrantz, Paul, and Vogel, Susan. Sex Role Stereotyping and Self Concepts in College Students. *Journal of Consulting and Clinical Psychology.* 32: 1968, 287-295.

12. Schramm, W., Lyle, J., and Parker, E.B. *Television in the Lives of Our Children.* Stanford, CA.: Stanford University Press, 1961, p. 25.

13. Surgeon General's Scientific Advisory Committee on Television and Social Behavior. *Television and Growing Up: The Impact of Televised Violence.* Washington, D.C. Government Printing Office, 1972.

14. Women on Words and Images, *Dick and Jane As Victims: Sex Stereotyping in Children's Readers,* 1972, P.O. Box 2163, Princeton, N.J. $2.00 pp.

MATERIALS USED IN STUDY

OBSERVATION FORM

Name of Show: All in the Family   Date: 11-10-73   Time: 8:00–8:3
Viewers: Stefan/Wilder   Channel: 2 – CBS

Number of Main Characters – Adult Male – 1 older, 1 younger
                                              Adult Female – 1 older, 1 younger

Number of Minor Characters – Adult Male – 1 middle age
                                                Adult Female – 2 middle age

Roles portrayed – Male – father, son-in-law, priest
                          Female – mother, daughter, neighbor, neighbor's sister

Occupations – Male – factory worker, student, priest
                     Female – housewife, works to support husband, nun

76

Description of situation	Sex of Char.	Trait exhibited
Opening scene — Archie and Edith singing together at piano	M/F	Affection
Gloria is cooking dinner as a surprise for family; horsemeat to save money — nutritious, economical, just like other meat	F	Initiative Intelligence
Michael objects strenuously to eating horse (big laughs)	M	Squeamishness
Gloria tricks Michael into eating a piece of meat	F	Manipulating
Michael runs to sink, screaming that he has eaten horse	M	Hysterical
Gloria: "C'mon Michael, I saw that look . . . you really liked it."	F	Manipulating
Michael admits he did like it.	M	Reasonable
Gloria reveals plan to serve horse to Archie and Edith, not tell them, Michael agrees	M/F	Manipulating
Edith thanks Gloria for cooking supper	F	Supportive
Michael sings "Camptown Races" (throughout show, continues to make innuendoes about meat — always gets big laughs)	M	Clever
Irene introduces her sister who is a nun — Edith replies to Michael's question about why Theresa is wearing street clothes, "Nowadays some nuns go around just like they was people."		
Archie enters, rude to Theresa, demands dinner	M	Domineering Rude
Michael leaves to help Gloria in the kitchen (at Gloria's request)	M	Helpful
Irene leaves with humorous exit line	F	Humor
Archie demands that Edith remove medal given her by Sister Theresa	M	Prejudice Domineering
Archie tells why he doesn't like Catholics	M	Prejudice
Irene and Theresa give serious explanation of Catholic faith	F	Intelligent
Archie retorts with put-down of Pope and Catholics	M	Stupidity Prejudice
Doorbell rings, Edith greets Father Majerski "You've grown a beard." Father Majerski: "Yes, I know." (big laugh) (Once again, Edith is made to look stupid.)	F	Stupidity
Father Majerski and Archie exchange insults	M	Derisive
Archie derides Gloria's effort to make supper: "It must be either the chink's or Colonel Saunders."	M	Derisive
Edith compliments Gloria on making supper	F	Kindness
Gloria whispers to Edith that meat is horse (so Archie can't hear)	F	Manipulating
Edith leaves table in horror	F	Squeamish

Description of situation	Sex of Char.	Trait exhibited
Gloria apologizes to mother for upsetting her	F	Affectionate
Edith says it's all right	F	Submissive need to conciliate
Edith describes day's events, gets jumped on by Archie who gets laughs for making fun of her	F	Victimized
Edith getting ready to leave gets made fun of by Archie who says she's running around like a loose weed	F	Victimized
Archie protests Edith's association with Catholics	M	Domineering Prejudiced
Archie visits Father Majerski, expresses fear that Edith will convert	M	Fear
Father Majerski tells Archie to talk to Edith himself	M	Intelligent
Father Majerski and Archie trade insults	M	Derisive
Archie tells Father Majerski to keep his hands off Edith or else	M	Threatening
Irene gets let in on the joke — horse for dinner — don't tell Archie	F	Manipulating
Archie calls Edith stupid for going to church	M	Derision
Irene retorts that that was dumb even for Archie	F	Assertiveness Defense of another
Archie gets really angry, waves finger in front of Edith's nose	M	Angry Domineering Authoritarian
Edith reassures Archie that she would never convert	F	Submissive
Irene defends Edith to Archie — important thing to love other people	F	Assertive Supportive
Michael affirms Irene's position — important to love other people	M	Supportive
Archie insults Michael	M	Derisive
Irene compliments Mike on Christian attitude	F	Supportive
Irene exits, saying she's glad the Protestants have Archie	F	Derisive
Archie tells Edith to leave the thinking to him, just do the useful things around here ... get me a beer.	M	Sexist
Edith complies	F	Submissive
Archie says he is hungry enough to eat a horse	M	Victimized

	No. M	No. F	Voiceover	Speaking part M – F	Occupations	What people are shown doing	Story line and/or sexist dialogue
Hill's Brothers'	2		M	–	bean expert	selecting coffeebeans	pride in family coffee business – only the best
Wrigley's Spearmint Gum	many	many	M	males singing Wrigley jingle	M band F baton twirlers all marching	all marching with large packs of gum	carry it with you – the big, fresh flavor.
VW	2			M	unknown	M pulls off VW cover M talks VW	VW owners' security blanket
Taster's Choice decaffeinated coffee		1		F	unknown	woman in night-gown is about to go to bed	"When Taster's Choice came out with their coffee, I said – but what about us decaf. drinkers? – And you know what? They heard me. Describes product. "Taster's Choice, thank you and good night".
Primatene Mist & tablets	1	1		M		speaker; flash to human model showing product's action	straight-forward appeal to asthma sufferers.
Lysol	1	1	M	M	unknown	pointing to places in kitchen where germs grow	Lysol kills odor causing germs in kitchen.
Anacin	1	0	M	M	unknown	talking to camera about pain relievers	diagram of headache is on female head.
Woolite	0	3	Female then male		unknown	posing in various wool outfits	appeal to women to wash their knits in Woolite. Knits are fashionable and Woolite washes them best.

Summary of Behaviors Observed for Male and Female for All Television Programs Analyzed

	Male		Female	
Behavior	Number of times observed	Percent of total behaviors	Number of times observed	Percent of total behaviors
1. Anger	165	13	77	10
2. Aggression	113	9	33	4
3. Cowardice	35	3	23	3
4. Incompetence	117	9	156	21
5. Dishonesty	63	5	54	7
6. Harming Physically	22	2	2	0
7. Emotionality	71	6	48	6
8. Jealousy	15	1	10	1
9. Non-Supportiveness	15	1	11	1
10. Self-Sacrifice	4	0	7	0
11. Discrimination	87	7	52	7
12. Using sexuality	11	0	12	2
13. Vanity	21	2	13	2
14. Warmth of Feeling*	48	4	23	3
15. Bravery*	21	2	2	0
16. Competence*	298	23	131	17
17. Honesty*	23	2	10	1
18. Humor*	38	3	10	1
19. Supportiveness*	107	8	87	11
Total Number of Behaviors	1274		761	

* Positive Behaviors

Note: (Aggression was considered negative. Positive aspects of aggressive behavior such as leadership or assertion were placed under competence).

Summary of Behaviors Observed for Male and Female for Adventure-Type Shows

	Male		Female	
Behavior	Number of times observed	Percent of total behaviors	Number of times observed	Percent of total behaviors
1. Anger	26	6	13	8
2. Aggression	46	11	8	4
3. Cowardice	7	2	14	8
4. Incompetence	14	3	53	31
5. Dishonesty	17	4	7	4
6. Harming Physically	10	2	2	1
7. Emotionality	14	3	20	12
8. Jealousy	5	1	2	1
9. Non-Supportiveness	3	0	0	0
10. Self-Sacrifice	1	0	0	0
11. Discrimination	16	4	14	8
12. Using Sexuality	0	0	5	3
13. Vanity	5	1	3	2
14. Warmth of Feeling*	12	3	0	0
15. Bravery*	13	3	2	1
16. Competence*	197	46	23	13
17. Honesty*	8	2	0	0
18. Humor*	3	0	0	0
19. Supportiveness*	27	6	6	3
Total Number of Behaviors	424		172	

* Positive Behaviors

OTHER RESOURCES

ORGANIZATIONS

Action for Children's Television (ACT). A pressure group working for more good programs and less exploitation of children on television. A one-year subscription to ACT's newsletter is $5.00 yearly. ACT, 46 Austin St., Newtonville, Mass., 02160.

Feminist Press. Publishes books for children as well as non-sexist curricular materials for elementary schools. Catalog available. Box 334, Old Westbury, N. Y. 11568.

KNOW, Inc. Publishes a wide variety of articles about the feminist movement. Catalog available. Box 86031, Pittsburgh, Pa. 15221.

National Organization for Women, 5 South Wabash St., Chicago, Ill. 60603. The major national organization for women's rights.

National Women's Political Caucus, 1921 Pennsylvania Ave. N.W., Washington, D. C. 20006.

Resource Center on Sex Roles in Education. National Foundation for the Improvement of Education. 1156 Fifteenth St. N.W. Washington, D. C. 20005.

Women's Action Alliance, 370 Lexington Ave., New York, N. Y. 10017. A group promoting non-sexist curricular materials.

Women's Equity Action League. Legislative action and information. 799 National Press Building, Washington, D. C. 20045.

Women on Words and Images. Along with publications, the group has slide shows on sex role stereotyping available for rental or purchase. ($40, $300.) Also provides consultants to conduct workshops on sexism in education or on television. P.O. Box 2163, Princeton, N. J. 08540.

BOOKS AND MAGAZINES

Books with Options. Boulder AAUW. 1056 Columbia Place, Boulder, Col., 80303. A bibliography of non-sexist children's books. $2.00.

Dick and Jane as Victims. By Women on Words and Images. $2.00 pp. Box 2163, Princeton, N. J. 08540.

Little Miss Muffet Fights Back. A bibliography of non-sexist books for children, by Feminists on Children's Media. $1.00. Order from Feminist Book Mart, 162-11 Ninth Ave., Whitestone, N. Y. 11357.

Journal of Communication, Spring, 1974. Vol. 24:2. Annenberg School of Communication, University of Pennsylvania, P.O. Box 13358, Philadelphia, Pa., 19101. Issue deals with women in television.

Media Reports to Women. 3306 Ross Place, N.W., Washington, D. C., 20008. A newsletter for media professionals.

MS. Magazine. Current information on feminism as well as monthly reviews of television programs. $10.00 yearly. MS., 370 Lexington Ave., New York, N. Y. 10017.

Sex Bias in the Public Schools. A report from New York NOW. $2.25. NYC NOW, 47 E. 19th St., New York, N. Y. 11220. Information also available on NOW TV study.

Sexism in Education. Emma Willard Task Force on Education, P.O. Box 14229, Minneapolis, Minn., 55414. A booklet for teachers $4.00.

Spokeswoman. A monthly newsletter. $7.00 yearly. 5464 South Shore Drive, Chicago, Ill. 60615.

The Psychology of Sex Differences. By Eleanor E. Maccoby. Stanford, CA.: Stanford University Press, 1974.

The Family Guide to Children's Television: What to Watch, What to Miss, What to Change and How to Do It. By Evelyn Kaye. New York: Pantheon, 1975.